Loaned

THE ARCHÆOLOGY OF PALESTINE
AND THE BIBLE

BASALT SLAB FROM BETH-SHAN, FIFTEENTH
CENTURY, B.C.

(By Permission of the University Museum)

The Richards Lectures delivered at the University of Virginia

The Archaeology of Palestine and the Bible

By
WILLIAM FOXWELL ALBRIGHT
*W. W. Spence Professor of Semitic Languages,
Johns Hopkins University, and Director of
the American School of Oriental Research in Jerusalem, 1920-1929*

NEW YORK CHICAGO
Fleming H. Revell Company
LONDON AND EDINBURGH

New York: 158 Fifth Avenue
Chicago: 851 Cass Street
London: 21 Paternoster Square
Edinburgh: 99 George Street

To
MY WIFE
who has borne
the burden
and the heat
of the day

FOREWORD

THE following pages are an expansion of the lectures delivered in February, 1931, at the University of Virginia, on the newly established Richards Foundation. Owing to the limitations of space, this book does not attempt to treat any phase of its subject exhaustively. In the first chapter we have tried to analyze the development of archæological research in Palestine, so as to make it intelligible to the layman; we have, therefore, laid stress on methods rather than on results. The second chapter presents a rapid sketch of the excavations at Tell Beit Mirsim, and describes the results somewhat more fully than in the very brief preliminary reports so far published. In the third chapter it is obviously impossible to discuss the subject of Archæology and the Bible fully, so we have selected certain aspects of it on which our own researches have thrown most light, or which seem to need a fresh treatment most urgently. Our point of view is neither strictly conservative nor liberal, and does not reflect the attitude of any special school of thought. In order to save the reader from being misled with regard to the bearing of archæological discovery, we have endeavoured to leave out personal views which are either not accepted by other scholars or which seem to us not ripe for publication.

The text of the book, including the notes, was completed in April, 1931. Some additional notes, covering the most important subsequent discoveries and publications, are appended (see *Addenda*).

W. F. A.

The Johns Hopkins University,
  Baltimore, Md.

TABLE OF ABBREVIATIONS

AJSL: American Journal of Semitic Languages and Literatures.

ANNUAL: Annual of the American Schools of Oriental Research.

AOTB: Altorientalische Texte und Bilder zum Alten Testament, second edition by Gressmann, Ranke, and Ebeling, 2 vols., Berlin, 1926–7.

BULLETIN: Bulletin of the American Schools of Oriental Research.

D: Deuteronomy, the Deuteronomic Code.

E: The Elohistic or Ephraimite Code.

EB: Early Bronze.

EI: Early Iron.

J: The Yahwistic or Judæan Code.

JAOS: Journal of the American Oriental Society.

JBL: Journal of Biblical Literature.

JE: The compilation of J and E.

JPOS: Journal of the Palestine Oriental Society.

JSOR: Journal of the Society of Oriental Research.

LB: Late Bronze.

MB: Middle Bronze.

P: The Priestly Code.

QS: The Quarterly Statement of the Palestine Exploration Fund.

RB: Revue Biblique.

ZAW: Zeitschrift für die Alttestamentliche Wissenschaft.

ZDPV: Zeitschrift des Deutschen Palästina-Vereins.

TABLE OF ARCHÆOLOGICAL PERIODS

Early Bronze I	cir.	3000–2600
Early Bronze II	"	2600–2300
Early Bronze III	"	2300–2000
Middle Bronze I	"	2000–1800
Middle Bronze II	"	1800–1600
Late Bronze I	"	1600–1400
Late Bronze II	"	1400–1200
Early Iron I	"	1200– 900
Early Iron II	"	900– 600
Early Iron III	"	600– 300

CONTENTS

I

THE DISCOVERY OF ANCIENT PALESTINE

1. RECENT PROGRESS IN PALESTINIAN ARCHÆOLOGY

IN the years since the close of the World War, there has been a striking revival of interest in archæological research. It is not our purpose to investigate the ultimate causes of this movement, in which America shares with the European nations. In part it may be parallel to the triumphant emergence of romanticism in art and literature, after a long eclipse. Wearied of an intellectual life which culminated in the mechanistic philosophy of war years, people of culture have altered their point of view so as to admit humanistic factors. The study of man, his past and his present, has gained a new importance, which is now expressing itself in the steady increase of endowments and foundations devoted primarily to it. Compared to these obscure, but irresistible tendencies of the day, other factors in the increase of interest in archæology are of minor importance. It is fortunate for archæology that American men of wealth have devoted themselves so widely to the collection of archæological objects; it is a happy coincidence that popular interest in the field was stimulated at so critical a period by the discovery of the tomb of Tut-ankh-aman. Yet events and tendencies like these are symptoms rather than causes.

Be that as it may, Biblical archæology has not been by any means the last to profit by the tendency of the times. In fact, it may be said to have profited by an exceptionally favourable combination of circumstances: the establishment of the British mandatory, with a well-organized Department of Antiquities and a liberal Antiquities Ordinance; the active interest taken by Mr. John D. Rockefeller, Jr., which has led to the excavation of Megiddo and the foundation of a magnificent Palestine Museum; the inauguration of a broad policy of coöperation on the part of the American School of Oriental Research in Jerusalem, which has greatly stimulated the launching of minor enterprises. The fact that Palestine is now governed as a British colony means that public security is generally better than in Ottoman times, and that the need of bribery in dealing with officials is very greatly reduced. Even more important to the archæologist is the presence of a certain number of men of high education and lofty ideals, which leavens the bureaucratic mass. The Department of Antiquities, supported by the international Archæological Advisory Board, controls the scientific responsibility of the scholars and institutions which conduct the work of excavation, and prevents native exploitation of ancient remains as far as possible. The first Director of Antiquities, Professor John Garstang of the University of Liverpool, himself an archæologist, directed several small excavations in person during his tenure of office. Since leaving the post, his interest in Palestine excavation has not flagged, but has shown itself in most fruitful researches and excavations, notably at Jericho. As a practical excavator, Garstang was able to understand the problems of the archæologist and to sympathize with his difficulties. His assistance to excavators greatly eased their task, and is gratefully remembered by all who dug in Palestine between the years 1920 and 1926. In 1927 he was followed by E. T. Richmond, Esq., who had won his spurs in administration rather than in archæology, though his work in the field of historical architecture and of Islamic art is of value. Shortly after Mr. Richmond's installation came the munificent Rockefeller gift of $2,000,000 for the establishment of a Palestine Museum of Archæology in Jerusalem. The construction and organization of this museum could not have fallen into better hands than those of Mr. Richmond. The administrative skill of the latter is also responsible for the solid organization of the Department of Antiquities along the lines marked out by Professor Garstang.

The second of the three circumstances which, as we observed, have combined to advance the cause of Biblical archæology in Palestine, is the attraction of Mr. Rockefeller's interest to archæology by Professor J. H. Breasted. Starting as an Egyptologist, the latter achieved an eminence in his chosen field which has brought him more international recognition than has ever before been accorded an American Orientalist. It was not until then that he founded the Oriental Institute of the University of Chicago, for which he received, in 1919, an annual subvention from Mr. Rockefeller. Thanks to Breasted's remarkable capacity for organization, as well as to his equally unusual ability to interest laymen in archæology, the Oriental Institute has continued to develop, with the aid of princely gifts from the Chicago Mæcenas, until it is now the most elaborate organization of its kind in the world, without even a remote competitor. Biblical archæology has benefited directly so far by the organization of the Megiddo excavation in 1925, followed in 1927 by the announcement of the gift for the Palestine Museum. This gift is divided into two parts: a million dollars for building, library, and equipment; a second million for endowment, since Palestine is much too poor to carry the operating expenses of so elaborate an institution without outside aid. It is expected that other enterprises will be launched by the Oriental Institute in Palestine and Syria during the coming years.[1]

Third in importance comes, we venture to maintain, the work of the American School in Jerusalem, which has directly stimulated the launching of a number of most productive minor undertakings, such as the excavations at Tell Beit Mirsim, Tell en-Naṣbeh, Bethshemesh, and Gerasa, to mention only a few. In 1929 this institution, together with its sister school in Baghdad, received the promise of half a million dollars from the Rockefeller Foundation. Half of this sum is to be paid to the Schools, to enable them to carry on their work on a much more solid basis during the years 1930–36, and the other half will be given to them as an endowment, at the expiration of this period, provided that an equal sum is contributed from outside for this purpose. Practically all American Oriental archæologists of standing, aside from the Egyptologists, are now directly or indirectly affiliated with the American Schools of Oriental Research. There can be no doubt that the further development of the Schools will greatly assist in the maintenance of high standards of archæological research.[2] It will also help materially to prevent the formation of a most undesirable cleavage between field archæologists and Oriental philologists, whose constant coöperation is essential to the progress of our research.

From this encouraging survey of the recent expansion and the future promise of the field of Palestinian archæology, let us turn to consider its intrinsic possibilities. First we must sketch its history, for without historical perspective, or as the natural scientists are coming to say, without a four-dimensional treatment, it is impossible to comprehend the evolution and the present tendencies of any science. Our title for this lecture, " The Discovery of Ancient Palestine," is not thoughtlessly purloined from the domain of physical geography. On the contrary, we describe the real discovery of the unknown past of the Holy Land. Like all lands of the Near East, its present is so very different from the historical past, that it is quite impossible to obtain a correct idea of any phase of the latter from the unaided study of the former. Except for the work of the last century, and especially of the last generation, it would be impossible to reconstruct the ancient social, political, or religious history, material civilization, arts and crafts, etc., since our chief documentary source, the Bible, invariably requires archæological elucidation before it becomes completely intelligible from any of these points of view.

The discovery of ancient Palestine is a two-fold task, which involves both surface exploration and excavation. The technique and methods employed by both types of archæological work have improved immeasurably since the beginning of scientific exploration in 1838, and of excavation in 1851. This first phase came to a close with the beginning of scientific excavation in 1890. The second phase, which lasted until the outbreak of the War in 1914, was, as we shall see, a period of collection and publication of material, which was not dated or classified with sufficient accuracy to make it of much value to the historian. During the third phase, since the close of the War, scientific method in the archæology of Palestine has improved so remarkably, and the amount of work accomplished has so increased that archæological data which were quite meaningless now yield important historical information. The progress of the linguistic study of ancient scripts and languages, not one of which could be read a century ago, has made it possible for the trained scholar to decipher all inscriptions found in Palestine, though written in many different scripts and an even greater number of tongues.

2. THE FIRST PHASE OF SCIENTIFIC EXPLORATION: ROBINSON AND HIS SUCCESSORS

We have said that the first phase began in 1838. It was in that year that Edward Robinson, a fellow American, undertook the first of his epoch-making journeys in Palestine, for the sake of studying its geography, topography, and archæological remains.[3] Robinson was just forty-four years of age when he began his fruitful travels in Palestine, but he had been admirably prepared for just such an enterprise. Raised on a New England farm, the son of a country minister, he had a background of physical strength, of culture, and of common sense and adaptability. He received his scholarly training in Germany, under some of the greatest scholars of the nineteenth century, the philologists Gesenius and Rödiger, the geographer Ritter, and the theologians Neander and

Tholuck. To round out his German training he married a German wife, the daughter of a professor, herself a woman of distinguished intellect. Robinson was not only the founder of the scientific topography of Palestine; he was also generally recognized as the foremost American Biblical scholar of his day in the fields of Hebrew and Greek linguistics and of Biblical interpretation. In only seven months of indefatigable travel on horseback, accompanied by his pupil and friend, Eli Smith, who had spent years in Syria as a missionary, he visited, described, and mapped many hundreds of modern villages and ancient sites, criticizing tradition with surgical ruthlessness, and proposing new identifications. Nearly all of his identifications of Biblical sites and most of his topographical observations have stood the test of time. Most important, however, was the combination of exhaustive study of all documents then available, and of critical examination of the tradition, with detailed and accurate personal observation and measurement. He was also the first Biblical topographer to record the exact form of modern Arabic place-names, a method which is now recognized as absolutely indispensable. No previous student had even combined two of these methods, to say nothing of uniting them all into a powerful scientific instrument for topographical research.[4]

We have dwelt at some length on the work of Robinson, not only because of its epochal importance, but because it illustrates so well the critical type of approach which is necessary if we are really to advance historical and archæological knowledge. It is not enough to know the land and the people, nor even to travel extensively and carry on excavation; one must also be trained to apply the most severely critical methods of historical, philological, linguistic, and comparative archæological analysis. It is not accidental that it was the great critical Semitist, Robertson Smith, who solved the main problems of the topography of Jerusalem long before the correct solutions became the common property of scholars, while all the leading authorities of the time, men intimately acquainted with Jerusalem and its antiquities, such as Wilson and Conder, held fast to now hopelessly antiquated conceptions.[5] The " authorities " scoffed at the supposed bookworm, but Robertson Smith's incisive analysis was right, whereas they were all wrong. Nor is it an accident that the best treatment of the historical and Biblical bearing of the archæological material discovered before the War in Palestine came from the pen of S. R. Driver, the greatest English Biblical scholar of modern times, who was much more of a bookworm than Robertson Smith.[6] We may also, in this connection, observe that the greatest ancient historian of modern times, Eduard Meyer, did not visit Crete, Egypt, Palestine, Syria, or Asia Minor until he was seventy-one years of age, and had never even visited an excavation until then. Yet his critical treatment of archæological discoveries was of the highest importance.

It would hardly seem necessary to point out the other side of the picture, since the value of a first-hand knowledge of the lands of the Bible and their archæology ought to be sufficiently obvious without a commentary. But it is generally second-rate scholars, not first-rate ones, who show the lack of such knowledge most painfully, since the latter are careful to verify their statements, familiarize themselves with the relevant literature, and apply to a reliable source for direct information when necessary.

In considering the surface exploration accomplished during the half century following Robinson's first visit to Palestine, one is struck by the lack of men of equal calibre, a lack which explains why, with all the activity in this field, there was hardly any progress—rather a recession—until after the lapse of a generation.[7] Again it was a single scholar of exceptional ability who turned the tide. This was Charles Clermont-Ganneau, who made his début as a young Orientalist of twenty-four, attached to the French Consulate in Jerusalem, by rescuing the Mesha Stone, menaced with destruction by the Arabs (1870). Before he was thirty Clermont-Ganneau had gained an international reputation for his brilliant archæological discoveries, showing a penetration and a sureness of method which far surpass the best that the archæology and topography of Palestine could exhibit before him. Among his more striking achievements were the solution of many difficult problems in epigraphy, the identification of the site of Gezer, as well as of a number of other ancient sites, and the demonstration that the notorious " Moabite antiquities " were barefaced forgeries, in which he was bitterly opposed by the leading German scholars of the day. It was somewhat later that he performed the still more sensational feat of proving the forgery of the Shapira manuscript of Deuteronomy, which purported to have been written by Moses himself, and was offered to Great Britain for the modest price of one million pounds sterling, which would now be equivalent in purchasing value to nearly fifteen million dollars.[8]

In 1865 the Palestine Exploration Fund was

founded, and as soon as possible proceeded to organize the Survey of Western Palestine, under the direction of competent army officers, including especially Kitchener [9] and Conder (1872–8).[10] In the maps and volumes of description which were duly published we have the basis for all subsequent archæological and topographic research.[11] This great work has not rendered further surface exploration superfluous; on the contrary, it has had the effect of stimulating it. There are many omissions, certain districts were not carefully studied, while the archæological importance of the *telûl* (plural of *tell,* " mound ") was only imperfectly understood at first, and many were omitted from the map; there are also many errors of orthography, which are generally the fault of the native scribe who was employed to write the name in Arabic. Moreover, no idea of the date of the ruins described could then be given, since the surveyors were army men, whose knowledge of archæology was very limited. Nor can they be blamed for their ignorance, since the most important criteria, especially the use of potsherds for dating, were not yet discovered.

During the first phase there were a number of excavations, but none were conducted according to scientific methods, as we now understand them. When de Saulcy cleared the so-called Tomb of the Kings, in 1851, his methods were precisely those of the treasure-hunter, and the critical archæological standards of the time may be gauged from the fact that he, one of the leading authorities of France, saw no difficulty in assigning the mausoleum in question to the time of the kings of Judah, nearly a thousand years too early. He considered the inscriptions on the sarcophagus of Queen Helena of Adiabene, a Parthian convert to

Judaism in the first century A. D., as referring to the consort of Zedekiah, more than six hundred years before—so little was then known of Hebrew and Aramaic epigraphy.[12]

Somewhat improved methods of digging, but yet prescientific in character, were introduced by Warren, who worked at Jerusalem for the recently established Palestine Exploration Fund from 1867 to 1870.[13] Neither he nor anyone else had any idea of the date of most of the masonry and small objects found in the vicinity of the Temple Area. Arabic geometric pottery was regarded as very ancient; the draughted stone blocks of the Herodian retaining wall, actually dating from the last decade before the birth of Christ, were considered to be Solomonic, *i. e.,* a thousand years older. When Warren attacked sites outside of Jerusalem, like Gibeah (Tell el-Fûl) and Jericho (Tell es-Sulṭân), he was perfectly helpless: the former he considered to be of Crusading date and of no interest, while the *tell* of the latter he supposed to represent a natural formation.[14]

The last excavation of any importance, disregarding the entirely unscientific operations carried out by various monastic orders in the hope of finding sacred objects and buildings, undertaken during this first phase, was the German work on the hill of Ophel, south of the Temple Area, under the direction of Guthe, later famous as an authority on the history and topography of Palestine. However, though measurements and elevations were more detailed and more careful than in any previous excavations in Palestine, no new methods were introduced, and Guthe had no idea of the date of most of the artifacts which he exhumed.[15]

3. THE SECOND PHASE OF SCIENTIFIC EXPLORATION: PRE-WAR EXCAVATIONS (1890–1914)

The year 1890 is a fateful date in the history of our subject, for it was then that W. M. Flinders Petrie undertook a six weeks' sounding in the mound of Tell el-Ḥesī, in southwestern Judah. During a number of years of productive excavation in Egypt, Petrie had begun to lay stress on the chronological value of pottery, hitherto neglected by archæologists, except in the case of painted Greek vases. Petrie was led to take an interest in Egyptian pottery through working with classical archæologists at the Græco-Egyptian site of Naucratis. After discovering that Egyptian pottery varied greatly in form and decoration during the centuries, he applied his new principles to work at Tell el-Ḥesī, where he dug scarp sections on the edge of the mound, and carefully noted the level at which every object was found. On comparing his results, he saw that the pottery of Palestine also varied greatly in character at different levels, and was thus able to set up a chronological scheme of pottery types, according to the level at which they were found.[16] The terminology proposed for the successive types of pottery was not at all bad; in fact it was in certain respects better than the nomenclature which was later introduced by Macalister. The ware belonging to what we now call Early and Middle Bronze (first phase) he termed " Amorite," while that of the Late Bronze was called " Phœnician." Macalister's names " Pre-Semitic, First Semitic," etc., were very misleading, and have now been entirely abandoned.

The next year (1891) an American scholar, Frederick Jones Bliss, the son of the distinguished president of the Syrian Protestant College, was appointed director of the excavations of the Palestine Exploration Fund at Tell el-Ḥesī, where he continued to dig for three campaigns (1891–3).[17] Clearing one-third of the deep, but small mound to bed-rock, Bliss distinguished eleven successive phases of occupation, which he assigned to eight separate strata of occupation, or "cities." Following Petrie, he distributed them over a period of about thirteen centuries, from about 1700 to about 400 B. C. The dates given to the strata by Bliss are substantially correct back to the end of the third city, thanks to numerous scarabs and a number of other inscriptions, cuneiform and Hebrew, found in them. The date of the first occupation must, however, be pushed back, with our present knowledge, to before 2300 B. C. Unfortunately, Bliss's publication of his results was inadequate, partly because of a mistaken policy of economy on the part of the Fund, so it was difficult for other scholars to obtain a clear idea of the ceramic classification and chronology. It is not surprising, therefore, that Conder, long head of the Survey of Western Palestine, scoffed at the idea of using common pottery for chronological purposes, nor that equal skepticism was expressed by Nowack, then the leading German authority on Biblical archæology.[18]

After an interlude at Jerusalem, where Bliss carried on excavations of considerable importance for our knowledge of the later topography of the city, he returned to the excavation of early mounds in 1898. For two years Bliss, assisted by a brilliant young English archæologist, R. A. S. Macalister, dug in four separate tells of the Shephelah, or low hill-country of Judah.[19] Though the work here was not of great significance, many small objects of interest were found, and the classification of pottery was materially improved, while the chronology offered in their publication (1902) was not superseded for some twenty years. In fact, owing to the circumstances attending later pre-War excavations, nearly all chronological systems proposed during this period represent a distinct regression.[20]

Bliss now resigned, to the lasting misfortune of Palestinian archæology, and was replaced by his associate, Macalister, who conducted five campaigns at the mound of Gezer (1902–09), a large *tell* in the low hill-country between Jerusalem and Jaffa.[21] Macalister's excavation was conducted very economically, and with extraordinary industry. In fact, despite his working single-handed, aside from the material help given him by the loyal and intelligent foreman, Yûsif Kanʿân, he was able to do all the surveying, planning, drawing and recording himself—a feat which no other excavator has equalled. To be sure, he only accomplished his work by devoting himself to the recording at the expense of adequate control. Moreover, economy dictated the use of the trench system. Long trenches, forty feet (twelve metres) wide, running north and south, were cleared to bed-rock, one after another, until eventually a considerable area had been excavated. Without adequate control of the work, it proved impossible either to distinguish with sufficient care between successive strata, or to produce continuous plans of any one stratum. It is vastly preferable to excavate areas instead of trenches, and to control the work by direct supervision, since even the best native foremen lack a real comprehension of what they are doing, and, therefore, employ a purely mechanical technique. Being alone, moreover, with no opportunity for comparing notes with associates, and lacking time to follow the work of other excavators, Macalister showed a very natural tendency toward shifting his chronology. In this case, as it happened, he shifted his chronology downward, so that " Persian " became " Hellenistic," while " pre-exilic " became " post-exilic " (Persian).

In spite of these handicaps, the results of the excavation of Gezer were of very great importance, and the publication of them in three large volumes was a monumental achievement for which Palestinian archæology must remain forever Macalister's debtor. Only to mention a few of the outstanding discoveries, we may refer to the troglodyte remains, which are still unique, the system of fortification employed at different periods, the great rock-hewn tunnel from the Middle Bronze, which provided the inhabitants of the city with direct access to a subterranean water-supply in time of siege. The high-place, or sanctuary of Gezer, with its *maṣṣebôth* and other cult-objects, still remains unique, since nearly all the other supposed high-places which have been excavated have been proved conclusively to have been purely profane installations, either stables, or private houses, in which the pillars served the purpose of supporting the floor of the second story, as well as of providing solid supports for tying up horses or for attaching looms, etc. The paucity of important public buildings, of sculptured objects, and especially of inscriptions in Macalister's excavation is due solely to the fact that he was unable to dig in the acropolis, on which stand a *welî* (saint's tomb) and cemetery. Below the acropolis he found an exceedingly rich group of sepulchral caverns, forming a royal necropolis of the Middle Bronze Age (cir. 1900–1700 B. C.).[22] If the acropolis of Gezer is ever excavated, there can be no question of the great wealth of material of direct historical value which will be discovered. However, even without touching the district of the city in which were the palaces and public buildings, Macalister was so fortunate as to find a number of valuable inscriptions in Hebrew and cuneiform, especially the calendar tablet, which, as we now know, dates from before 900 B. C., and is thus considerably older than the Mesha Stone.[23]

About the same time that Macalister began digging at Gezer, a German Biblical scholar, Ernst Sellin, commenced excavations in northern Palestine, which had not yet been touched by the Palestine Exploration Fund. Under Austrian auspices he dug at Tell Ta'annek, the site of ancient Taanach, in 1901 and 1903.[24] The mound is rich in antiquities, and his discoveries were of exceptional importance, though the archæological methods were primitive when compared to those which are now employed. The most remarkable find was in the palace of 'Ashtar-yashur,[25] where, among other objects, no fewer than a dozen cuneiform tablets, probably from the sixteenth century B. C., at least a century before the date of the Amarna Tablets,[26] came to light. Most of these tablets were actually recovered in 1903, in sifting the débris removed in 1901 from the ruins of the palace. In the hands of linguists and philologists, these tablets have yielded very important information with regard to the condition of Canaan at that time, politically, ethnically, and culturally.[27] A cuneiform cylinder seal, with mixed Mesopotamian and Egyptian decoration, belonging to a certain Atanakhilī, son of Khabsum, who lived before 1800 B. C., shows at how early a date this script was used in Palestine. The historical results obtained from the unwritten material examined in the course of the excavation were very disappointing, because of the lack of satisfactory ceramic chronology. Because of what appeared to be adequate evidence, the dates of strata were reduced in each case by from one to three centuries. It must be said, however, that Sellin himself was very cautious in drawing conclusions.

German interest in Palestinian archæology, thus successfully aroused, was whetted by the inauguration of work at Tell el-Mutesellim, the site of ancient Megiddo, perhaps better known as Armageddon, under the auspices of the Deutscher Palästina-Verein, and the direction of G. Schumacher (1903–05).[28] Schumacher, who was a civil engineer by profession, and who had surveyed most of Eastern Palestine for the Palestine Exploration Fund and the Palästina-Verein, had not had much experience in excavating, and knew practically nothing about pottery. Moreover, he was forced to work with practically no assistance, because of the desire for economy. It is, therefore, not surprising that stratigraphy was neglected, and that the treatment of the pottery was entirely inadequate. The old trench system was followed throughout, though perhaps this method of excavation was hardly avoidable at a time when sensational discoveries appeared to be the only means of keeping the interest of the public awake, and of securing funds for further work. As a matter of fact, however, the trenching method actually had precisely the opposite effect, since an unkind Fate pre-

vented Schumacher from making any discovery of
major importance, though several have already been
made by the Americans who have followed in his
wake since the War. The most remarkable single
discovery made by him was at the very outset, when
a beautiful jasper seal, bearing the representation of
a lion rampant, with the name of its owner, " Shema',
officer of Jeroboam," came to light. This seal belongs
to the time of Jeroboam II, who reigned over the
Northern Kingdom in the first half of the eighth
century B. C. It was valued at $10,000, and deposited
for safety in the royal treasury of the Sultan of
Turkey.[29]

In 1907 Sellin began a new excavation, with Austrian support, at Tell es-Sulṭân, the site of ancient
Jericho, and for two well organized campaigns
(1908–09), the undertaking was carried on under the
auspices of the Deutsche Orient-Gesellschaft.[30] Sellin
and a classical archæologist, C. Watzinger, directed
the excavation, with the assistance of trained archi-
tects. Since Harvard began work at Samaria in 1908,
we may consider that year as a turning point in the
history of Palestinian archæology. It was thenceforth
considered as necessary to staff the expeditions at
work in the field sufficiently so that the recording of
results would not be neglected. How important this
is will be evident as soon as we recall that the excavator must destroy ancient remains in order to reach
the remains below; it is then forever too late to control his description of the material which has been
destroyed.

In spite of the greatly improved technique, and the
care devoted to recording, the trench system was employed, and the stratification was, accordingly, not

definitively established. Moreover, Sellin's initial error in chronology, at Taanach, was now magnified into a mistake of some six or eight hundred years, which led to the paradoxical attribution of the latest Middle Bronze stratum, dating a century or two before the end of the Canaanite occupation, to the age of the Israelite reoccupation of Jericho, under Hiel the Bethelite, in the reign of Ahab (cir. 860 B. C.).[31] But, despite this confusion in chronology, the German excavators surpassed all their predecessors in the precision and completeness of their engineering treatment, and the published account of the successive fortifications of the town is a model of scientific method, which forms the basis to-day for all study of the Canaanite art of building city walls. The excellence of this phase of their work was to be shown by the results of the excavations carried on in 1929 by Garstang, of which more anon.

America, which had furnished Robinson, and which had sent Bliss to continue Petrie's work, now took the field on her own account, with an elaborately organized and very successful expedition from Harvard University, for the purpose of digging the site of Samaria (1908–10).[32] Thanks to the liberality of the late Jacob Schiff, who gave the then magnificent sum of $60,000 for the excavation of Samaria, the enterprise was well supported.[33] Thanks to the fact that it was directed for most of the time by George A. Reisner, who was later to be recognized as the best field archæologist working in Egypt and Western Asia, the excellence of the methods employed was assured. The architect of the expedition was C. S. Fisher, who was also to become one of the foremost field archæologists of our time. This important undertaking is now being resumed (spring of 1931) by Harvard, and brilliant discoveries may confidently be awaited. The outstanding find of the pre-War excavation was a complex of ruins containing the remains of successive palace constructions of Omri, Ahab, and a third monarch whose identity remains doubtful.[34] In the ruins of the age of Ahab was discovered a collection of several hundred inscribed potsherds, which, after being fitted together so far as possible, proved to belong to some seventy separate ostraca. These ostraca are written in ink, in old Hebrew characters, and contain various data with regard to the nature and provenience of shipments of wine and oil to Samaria. In other words, they are dockets belonging to payments of taxes in kind by districts and towns in the province of Manasseh. On superficial perusal, nothing would seem any less interesting or instructive, but a systematic study, by several scholars, has shown that they are documents of very great value.[35] They throw light, for example, on the language and religion of the Northern Kingdom, on its topography, and especially on its provincial and its fiscal organization, of which very little was previously known. We now know, for instance, that the official language of Samaria in the time of Elijah and Elisha was different from Biblical Hebrew, which from other inscriptions we know to have been the language of Jerusalem. The ostraca also set the tribal and clan organization of Israel in an entirely new light, which enables us to understand the political evolution of Israel better. Most important of all is the new material for the fiscal administration of Israel, but consideration of it is not in place here.

No royal inscriptions on stone were found in the

pre-War excavations at Samaria, but we may confidently expect them to be discovered by the new expedition. That the kings of Israel were accustomed to erect stelæ with inscriptions recounting their deeds may be taken for granted, since it was the ordinary practise of the day. The very first such stela found in Syria, the famous Moabite Stone, belonged to Mesha king of Moab, who rebelled successfully against Israel after Ahab's death. Since Moab had been tributary to Israel for about a century and a half, we may be sure that the Moabites employed Israelite customs as well as the Israelite language.[36]

Further excavations in Samaria will also throw much light on the problem of the fortifications of the Israelite city, which was not solved by Reisner and Fisher before the War. They will also yield important material from the so-called Babylonian period of Samaria's history, which followed the capture of the city by the Assyrians in 721.[37] It will be recalled that Samaria then became the capital of an Assyrian province, and remained a district capital until the Greek period. In the Persian age it was the capital of the Sanballat family, which professed a paganizing type of Judaism, and opposed the reforms of Nehemiah and Ezra.[38] Herod the Great completely rebuilt Samaria, calling it Sebaste in honour of the Emperor Augustus. The history of Roman Samaria extends from just before the birth of Christ to the Byzantine age. Very interesting finds have already been made in the ruins of this period, and many more may be expected.[39]

After a long interval of neglect excavation was resumed at Jerusalem in 1909. Unfortunately, it was not a serious enterprise, but a frank search for treasure which was now undertaken by an English syndicate, under the direction of Captain Parker. A permit was secured with ease from the Ottoman Porte, money was spent right and left, and excavations were begun on the hill of Ophel, the site of Canaanite Jerusalem, just south of the Temple Area. An erratic Finnish savant, one Juvelius, claimed to have found in the book of Ezekiel a cipher which gave the true location of the Temple treasure, concealed at the Babylonian Exile. A Danish adventurer, a clairvoyant, joined the expedition, and directed its operations by crystal-gazing. After two years spent in aimless probing, with no discovery of treasure, Parker turned to the Temple Area itself, bribed the Turkish governor of Jerusalem, the head sheikh of the Dome of the Rock (the notorious Khalîl ed-Danaf), and other officials, and conducted secret excavations during the night. Such proceedings could not long be concealed; a disgruntled workman divulged the secret, and the excitement among the Moslems of Jerusalem and the surrounding area was so intense that a general massacre of the Christians seemed imminent. Parker fled in haste, reaching his yacht at Jaffa just in time to escape arrest. The Constantinople authorities promptly deposed and imprisoned the officials whom Parker had bribed. Unfortunate as was the impression created everywhere by this scandalous episode, scholars were not entirely ungrateful. Parker cleared out many rock-cut tunnels and caves, in which he made interesting discoveries of very early Canaanite pottery. Happily for science, Père Vincent, already known to specialists as the foremost authority on the archæology and topography of Jerusalem, was able to secure from Parker, who was a gentleman, whatever his defects as a scholar, permission to follow the work of the expedition and to record its results. Needless to say, he availed himself fully of this permission, and subsequently published full accounts of the results.[40] The tunnels and water-shafts discovered by Parker provided Vincent with material for a complete reconstruction of the complicated history of the engineering enterprises by which the ancient inhabitants of the city assured themselves of a water-supply from the Fountain of the Virgin, even in the time of siege. The exterior opening of the spring was covered and concealed, while the water was diverted into subterranean tunnels, communicating with the city by oblique or vertical shafts. Parker's work proved to the satisfaction of all scholars of standing that the oldest Canaanite and Israelite Jerusalem really stood on the southeastern, not on the western hill; it also proved that Jerusalem was founded many centuries before the time of Abraham.[41]

Passing over the few remaining excavations in Palestine before the fateful year 1914,[42] since none of them were of outstanding significance, we come to the War years, when no field work could be carried on, but when scholars and historians had at last a breathing space, in which they could attempt to correlate and synthetize the data collected since 1890. In 1916 Handcock published a book entitled *Archæology of the Holy Land,* in which he tried to present a systematic, chronologically arranged outline of Palestinian archæology. The confusion in it is indescribable. The dates given by Sellin and Watzinger for Jericho, those given by Bliss and Macalister for the mounds of the Shephelah, by Macalister for Gezer, and by Mackenzie for Beth-shemesh do not agree at all, and the attempt to base a synthesis on their chronology resulted, of course, in chaos. Moreover, most of the excavators failed to define the stratigraphy of their site, and thus left its archæological history hazy and indefinite, with a chronology which was usually nebulous where correct, and often clear-cut where it has since been proved wrong. Small wonder that historians and Biblical scholars turned away from this chaos of conflicting views in despair, convinced that the main purpose of archæology was to unearth inscriptions, and occasionally to elucidate the arts and crafts of the ancient inhabitants.

4. EXCAVATIONS SINCE THE WAR

In 1917 General Allenby entered Jerusalem and freed the Holy City from the domination of Islam. The following year came his brilliant encircling movement, by which he drove the Turks from Samaria, and shortly afterwards swept them from Galilee as well. In 1920 the British established civil government in Palestine, and the first High Commissioner, Sir Herbert Samuel, at once created a Department of Antiquities, under the direction of John Garstang, well and favourably known for his excavations in Egypt, Ethiopia, and Syria. Garstang lost no time in beginning excavations himself, on behalf of the Palestine Exploration Fund, which was thus the first organization to reënter the field which it had first cultivated. The third phase of the history of Palestinian archæology now commences. Under the new conditions, which we have described briefly above, archæological work has been encouraged by the government, instead of being discouraged by oppressive laws and a venal bureaucracy. The new Antiquities

Ordinance, which assures the excavator a fair proportion, generally about half, of the objects which he unearths, has attracted museums into the field. The comparative ease with which responsible scholars or institutions can now obtain permits to excavate has led to a great increase in small undertakings. However, most important of all has been the change in the spirit of the times, to which we alluded at the beginning of this lecture, a spirit favourable to the expansion of archæological activity.

The number of new enterprises, most of which are not finished, and few of which are yet definitively published, is so great that an attempt to describe them all would be very confusing. We shall, accordingly, limit ourselves to a sketch of the most important undertakings, and lay stress on the development of method rather than on isolated discoveries. Slow at first, the progress of coöperation and synthesis has been increasingly rapid, especially since about 1925, so that we may now speak of a definite consensus of scholarly opinion, the conclusions of which are being subjected to new tests every year. It is hardly necessary to say that, being based on a long process of induction, these results are seldom modified by comparison with new inductions. It is, on the other hand, true that the success already attained in interpreting the material unearthed by excavators constitutes a danger for future scholars, who may try to apply similar methods without adequate methodological preparation. The same thing happened after the brilliant achievements of the linguists and philologists of the past century, in comparing known languages and deciphering new ones. Some scholars of proved ability and many more dilettanti rushed into the newly opened territory with immature theories and wild hypotheses, whose publication, often accompanied by popularization, has given " philology " a bad name in many quarters, undeserved though this reputation is.

The human factor cannot be neglected in studying the history of any science. In Palestinian archæology it plays its usual rôle. Without the close relations now existing between archæologists and other scholars in Palestine, and without the continuity of method and of knowledge which is ensured by the presence of such men as Père Vincent and C. S. Fisher, our science could not possibly make the rapid strides which we observe. The French École Biblique de St. Étienne, recognized by the French Government after the War as one of its official schools of archæology, with a galaxy of distinguished scholars, Fathers Lagrange, Vincent, Abel, Jaussen, Savignac, Dhorme, to mention only a few of the best known among its faculty, has served as a notable archæological focus.[43] We may also claim that the American School of Oriental Research, with its constant stress on coöperation between different institutions, as well as between religious and national groups, which has found concrete expression in the Palestine Oriental Society,[44] has exerted a useful influence in the direction of collaboration and continuity of scholarly effort. The Hebrew University[45]; the German Evangelical School, under the successive direction of Dalman and Alt[46]; the British School, long submerged in the Department of Antiquities, but now independent[47]; the Pontifical Biblical School,[48] and other less important institutions are all coöperating in the friendliest fashion. All these institutions represent foci of continuous interest. Another, in some respects even more important factor in producing continuity of research is the elaborate and solidly organized work of the Oriental Institute of the University of Chicago at Megiddo, and of the University of Pennsylvania Museum at Beth-shan. Even when directors are changed, the plant and the organization remain, while the accumulating records form a steadily increasing mass of accurate information. It is precisely in such elaborate organizations, however, that the human factor suffers most, and the disadvantages of the machine method become most evident. In an elaborate undertaking, the director is often so submerged under a mass of routine duty, most of which has only an indirect relation to the actual excavation and interpretation, that he has scant time and energy left for his scholarly work. Under such conditions the excavation itself may fall almost entirely into the hands of native foremen, who are trained to follow certain arbitrary methods, but naturally have no comprehension of the meaning and purpose of what they are doing. Bruno Meissner has wisely said that no amount of technical organization can replace an intelligent mind.[49] This principle is the great justification of small and simply organized archæological undertakings, which should naturally restrict themselves to small sites, and not attempt large mounds like Megiddo and Beth-shan.

5. THE EXCAVATION OF BETH-SHAN

There is no object in following a strictly chronological order in dealing with the excavations of post-War years. It is much simpler to describe the results of the most important undertakings, roughly following the order of their significance. Let us, therefore, begin with the work of the University of Pennsylvania

Museum at Beth-shan, under the successive direction
of C. S. Fisher (1921–3), Alan Rowe (1925–8), and
G. M. Fitzgerald (1930—).[50] We need not dwell on
the relatively unimportant discoveries made in the
upper strata, extending in time from the Ptolemaic
period to the age of Saladin, about fifteen hundred
years. Below the Hellenistic level the excavators at
once found themselves in remains dating back to before 1000 B. C., when David destroyed the city, never
occupied again until some seven centuries later. The
real interest of Beth-shan to the archæologist begins
when he has penetrated down into the strata which
antedate the end of the second millennium B. C. No
fewer than five separate strata from the second millennium B. C. have so far been examined over a
respectable area, the five levels extending from the
fifteenth century down to about 1000 B. C. It is impossible to offer more than a guess as to the number of
strata still untouched, or as to the age when the town
was founded. Since its situation is extraordinarily
advantageous from the point of view of the first builders of towns in this region, offering as it does an
unlimited water supply for irrigation, as well as beautiful plains to irrigate, it is not unreasonable to suppose
that it was founded before the end of the chalcolithic,
that is, before 3000 B. C.

The lowest stratum so far studied at Beth-shan may
be dated accurately to the reign of Pharaoh Tuthmosis
III (cir. 1501–1447 B. C.), thanks to many scarabs
bearing his name, as well as to other adequate indications. In this level Rowe made a number of very remarkable discoveries in the campaigns of 1927 and
1928. A great temple-complex containing two sanctuaries was almost completely uncovered; both were

built of adobe brick, but the ground-plan of the walls
could be traced throughout. A broken limestone stela
found in the southern sanctuary proved that it belonged to the god Makal, called " god of Beth-shan "
on inscriptions. The name Makal is practically synon-
ymous with the better known Rashap (Resheph), the
name of the Canaanite god of the underworld, who
was both god of fertility and god of pestilence and
destruction, these two opposing aspects being characteristic of ancient chthonic divinities.[51] Curiously
enough, we do not find the name of Makal mentioned
again in our fragmentary inscriptional sources until
the fourth century B. C., when it appears in the com-
pound name Rashap-Makal, identified by the Cypriotes
with their own Apollo. The northern temple was
evidently sacred to the goddess consort of Makal,
probably the 'Anat who was worshipped with Rashap
in the two temples of Beth-shan excavated by Rowe
in the Ramesside stratum. In the temple-complex were
found a great many articles, both votive offerings and
cult objects, illustrative of the religion and culture of
the Canaanites. From the standpoint of Biblical history, the fifteenth century falls between the Patriarchal
Age in the narrow sense and the Age of Moses, and
accordingly illustrates both. The most interesting
single find was a large basalt slab with the representation of a combat between a lion and a mastiff, in
low relief.[52] In the upper register the two animals
stand on their hind legs, facing one another; in the
lower one the lion is shown standing, with his mouth
open in the act of roaring, while the mastiff attacks
his hind quarters. Though this slab evidently served
as an orthostat, that is, as a casing for the lower part
of a brick wall or pier, no other similar slab was dis-

covered, so it may have been imported from the north.
It is, at all events, by far the most artistic object yet
found in any Canaanite level in Palestine, aside, of
course, from the many articles of Egyptian manufacture. If we could be sure of its Canaanite prove-
nience, our respect for Canaanite art would immediately rise, but there is reason, as just observed, to
suspect a northern origin, in Syria or northern Mesopotamia. The closest parallels so far discovered are
the still unpublished slabs and sculptures excavated
by Baron von Oppenheim at Tell Ḥalâf, Biblical
Gozan, in northern Mesopotamia. While the date of
his extraordinary finds is still doubtful, they appear
to be rather older than the Beth-shan slab. At all
events, the material from Tell Ḥalâf proves conclusively that those authorities who would depress the
date of our slab by several centuries are wrong. That
they are wrong can be stated apodictically by those
who are conversant with the stratification of the
mound at the point where the slab was found.

Just to the south of the inner shrine of the Makal
sanctuary, Rowe found a room containing an altar
of sacrifice.[53] On the top of the altar is an L-shaped
channel, eight inches wide and deep, by which the
blood of the sacrificial animal was carried away from
the altar. In the channel on the altar is a hole for
the wooden peg to which the animal was tethered
before it was slaughtered. Against the south side of
the altar were found lying the two horns of a bull
which had been sacrificed on the altar. In the courtyard, just to the west of the altar steps, was found
the collar bone of a bull, presumably of the same animal, which was about three years of age, together with
a dagger of bronze, presumably employed in the

sacrifice.[54] We have here a vivid picture of the last
sacrifice offered in the temple of Makal before the
citadel of Beth-shan was destroyed—by whom we do
not know. Other similar discoveries made in the
temple-complex of the Tuthmosis III stratum enable
us to visualize many other details and aspects of
Canaanite religion, about which virtually nothing was
known prior to these excavations. At the same time
we are able to gain a much better idea both of the
similarities and of the much greater differences between Canaanite and Israelite religion.

The four subsequent strata could all be dated by
scarabs, inscriptions on stone, and other objects, with
a precision never equalled in the previous history of
Palestinian excavations. For this reason, the excavations at Beth-shan are of the very greatest value to
the archæologist, since they enable him to date pottery
and other artifacts of the same period when found
in other sites without dated inscriptions to fix their
exact place in time. After the level of the time of
Tuthmosis III comes one from the second half of the
fifteenth century, followed by a level belonging to the
reign of Amenophis III (1411–1375 B. C.). Then
comes a stratum from the time of Sethos I of the
Nineteenth Egyptian Dynasty, itself divided into two
building levels, one above the other. Then, lastly, we
reach a very thick level, which extends from the reign
of Ramesses the Great (1292–1225 B. C.) to the
destruction of Beth-shan by the Israelites. From the
Bible, which states that Beth-shan was still standing,
in Philistine hands, at the death of Saul, and from
the total absence of any remains on the mound which
can be dated between the tenth and the fourth centuries
B. C., it becomes practically certain that it was cap-

tured and destroyed by David, shortly after 1000 B. C.[55]

In the Ramesside stratum were found two very interesting basalt stelæ, one belonging to the first year of Sethos I (cir. 1315 B. C.), the second to the ninth year of Ramesses II (cir. 1284 B. C.). The monument of Sethos contains a very important account of a military campaign in which the Pharaoh suppressed an incipient revolt in the Beth-shan area; the town is mentioned twice in the text, which incidentally settles a number of difficult questions of topography. The great monument of Ramesses II, nine feet high, contains a long inscription replete with boasts and empty phrases. Interesting to the Bible student is a reference to the town of Ramesses, Biblical Raamses, which the Israelites were said to have built during their Egyptian bondage.[56] In his first campaign Dr. Fisher found another inscription of Sethos I in the Byzantine level, where it had been reused as a door lintel. This inscription is unhappily preserved only in part, so the historical data to which it alludes remain tantalizingly obscure. Most unfortunate is the vagueness of the reference to the 'Apiru people, evidently the Khabiru of the Amarna Tablets, and generally believed to represent the Biblical Hebrews.[57]

In the same stratum was found a basalt statue of Ramesses III, the last Pharaoh of the New Empire to maintain any hold over the Asiatic dependencies of Egypt. The statue is very poorly executed, a fact which illustrates the decline of Egyptian prestige. It was in this reign that the Philistines invaded Palestine and settled in the Coastal Plain, regardless of Egyptian opposition (cir. 1170 B. C.).[58]

6. MEGIDDO

The second most important archæological enterprise launched in Palestine since the War is beyond dispute the excavation of Megiddo by the Oriental Institute of the University of Chicago, organized by J. H. Breasted. This expedition began work in 1925, under the direction of C. S. Fisher, followed in 1927 by P. L. O. Guy, and now represents the high-water mark of comprehensive and efficient organization in a Palestinian excavation.[59] The entire site of Tell el-Mutesellim has been acquired by purchase, and the mound is being removed systematically, stratum by stratum, level by level. This method has been the ideal of most American excavators, but it has only been applied without modification at Megiddo. Against it may be said, to be sure, that complete removal of a mound prevents future archæologists, with improved methods, from supplementing and correcting the results of previous excavators. When, on the other hand, it is properly carried out, under careful supervision by a competent man, this method assures us of complete and coherent plans, and exhaustive records, which possess a cumulative power of demonstration. Fortunately, both methods of excavation, complete and partial clearance, have their advocates, and both will continue to be followed. The only method which is justly falling into disrepute is that of trenching, for which there is little to be said except on the ground of practical necessity.

A great undertaking like that at Megiddo is slow in getting under way, so comparatively few remarkable discoveries may as yet be chronicled. Four strata have so far been examined, extending backward from the fourth century B. C. to the tenth. The upper two, dating from the Babylonian and Persian periods, belonged to unimportant villages, in whose ruins practically nothing of interest was found. The third stratum, of the seventh century B. C., yielded more interesting remains, especially in the ruins of a small temple or sanctuary of Astarte, Biblical Ashtaroth. Here were found altars of incense, Astarte figurines, and proto-Ionic capitals, all showing the extremely intimate relation between Phœnicia and Israel at that time. It was reserved for Mr. Guy to make one of the most remarkable finds ever made in Palestine, which has illuminated a period regarding which archæology has had very little to say, the age of Solomon. In the absence of archæological illustration it was easy to speak contemptuously about this age, and to suggest that Solomon was really a very insignificant ruler, even judged by the standards of that day. In the fourth stratum, belonging to the early monarchy of Israel, Guy found in 1928–9 well-built stone stables for some three hundred horses, together with space for chariots and grooms. The stables were constructed of hewn stones, with the long, rectangular shape which we have learned to associate with the tenth and ninth centuries B. C. in Israel. This type of masonry was undoubtedly introduced into Palestine from outside, probably from Phœnicia, in the reign of Solomon, whose relations with Hiram of Tyre were so intimate.[60] Running lengthwise of the stables were two rows of massive pillars of stone, serving both as supports for the roof and as tie-posts. Between the pillars were stone feed-troughs, and the floor of the stables, especially between the two rows of pillars, was paved with hydraulic lime plaster as hard as cement. The alleys and courts between the stables were also covered with the same hard plaster. According to I Kings 10:26 ff. (cf. 9:15–19) Solomon built chariot cities in which to keep his twelve thousand chariot horses, since cavalry horses were not used in those days [61]; Megiddo is one of the places mentioned in this connection. The splendour of the great king's reign, and the care with which he provided for the horses which he imported into Israel for the first time are both vividly illustrated by the discoveries at Megiddo.

7. MINOR AMERICAN EXCAVATIONS

American enterprise is also responsible, aside from the two major undertakings which we have just described, for a number of successful minor excavations initiated by the American School of Oriental Research in Jerusalem. The first excavation was undertaken in 1922–3 by the School itself, under the writer's direction, on the mound of Tell el-Fûl, the site of Gibeah of Benjamin, the home and residence of Saul, first king of Israel.[62] A very ancient fortress (*migdal,* rendered "tower" in the English Bible) was examined, and proved to contain four different strata, and seven different phases of building, commencing at the very outset of Israelite history, about 1200 B. C., and closing in the early Roman period, about the first century A. D. The first stratum, from the time of the Judges, had been burned, as described in the Bible (Jud. 20:40). This confirmation of the Biblical narrative is particularly interesting, since the historicity of the story in question has often been doubted. The second fortress belonged to the time of Saul himself (end of eleventh century B. C.), and exhibited very solid masonry and a considerable amount of rustic wealth. We must, of course, remember that Saul remained essentially a wealthy peasant, even after his coronation, and that his power was extremely limited.

In 1924 the American School began a series of joint expeditions, which were directed by the writer, in close coöperation with Dr. M. G. Kyle, then president of Xenia Theological Seminary. The first of these coöperative expeditions carried us down to the southern end of the Dead Sea, and the adjacent land of Moab.[63] Our most important find, in this campaign of exploration, was a very large camping ground and fortress from the latter part of the Early Bronze, at Bâb ed-Drâ'.[64] While we have not yet been able to excavate it, our surface discoveries provided all that was necessary to give us a clear idea of the age and the purpose of this installation. Taken in conjunction with our archæological survey of the southern Dead Sea valley, the Bâb ed-Drâ' fortress and camp provide us for the first time with a chronological basis for fixing the date of the destruction of the Early Bronze culture of Sodom and Gomorrah, so vividly recounted in Genesis 19.[65] The results of this and numerous other expeditions made by the writer into the Jordan Valley have definitively established the correctness of the very early Biblical tradition that the valley was very prosperous and densely peopled when Abraham came into the country.[66] The population of the Jordan Valley decreased steadily thereafter, partly because of the catastrophe described in Genesis, and reached the lowest point in its history in the Israelite period, about 900 B. C.[67]

In 1926 we began the joint excavation of Tell Beit Mirsim, probably Biblical Debir, or Kiriath-sepher.

So far we have devoted three campaigns (1926, 28, 30) to this task; Dr. Kyle and the writer hope to undertake the fourth campaign in 1932. Since the second chapter will be concerned with this excavation, we need not dwell on it here.

In the same year Dr. W. F. Badè, of the Pacific School of Religion, began excavation at Tell en-Naṣbeh, seven miles north of Jerusalem, and regarded by many scholars as the site of Biblical Mizpah.[68] This expedition was organized with the help of Fisher, who has been associated with the School as professor of archæology since 1925, and whose influence on the scientific character of American excavations in Palestine has been very beneficial indeed. Badè has so far conducted three campaigns at Tell en-Naṣbeh (1926, 27 and 29), and has succeeded in examining practically the entire surface of the mound, a feat possible only because of the shallowness of the débris of occupation.[69] The most remarkable discovery at this site has been, without doubt, the extraordinarily massive city wall, which averages some seventeen feet (five metres) in thickness, and in one place reaches the width of twenty-six feet. At more or less regular intervals the wall was strengthened by towers, the base of which was protected by sloping stone revetments. This wall belongs to the Middle Bronze Age, and was repaired during the Iron Age by the Israelites, perhaps to serve as an outpost of the Northern Kingdom against Judah.[70]

In 1928 Elihu Grant of Haverford College began excavations at Tell er-Rumeileh, or 'Ain Shems, the site of the Biblical Beth-shemesh.[71] Work had been begun here before the War by the Palestine Exploration Fund, under whose auspices Duncan Mackenzie

dug for three short campaigns (1911–12), which were
mostly devoted to a Byzantine monastery and to the
clearance of Israelite tombs.[72] The Fund generously
ceded its rights of priority to Grant, who began work
with Fisher's help, and has continued to work every
year since (third campaign 1930). The town was
founded, it would appear, in the seventeenth century
B. C., during the Hyksos Age, and was occupied continuously down to the Babylonian Captivity, some
eleven centuries.[73] Four strata have been distinguished, all of which overlap archæological periods,
a fact which increases the difficulty of the work at the
same time that it enhances its interest. Grant has been
remarkably fortunate in comparison with Mackenzie;
at the outset of his work his pickmen broke into two
large sepulchral caverns which proved to be literally
full of fine pottery, weapons, jewelry, scarabs, etc.,
from the Late Canaanite and Early Israelite periods.
At the end of his third campaign he found a sherd
inscribed in ink (ostracon), in Old Hebrew characters,
and dating from not later than the fourteenth century
B. C. Showing the great antiquity of writing in Palestine, and carrying back the use of the Hebrew script
to a period antedating Moses, this discovery has naturally made a sensation.[74]

8. BRITISH ARCHÆOLOGICAL UNDERTAKINGS

The Palestine Exploration Fund was actually, as
we have said, the first organization to reënter the field
of Palestinian archæology after the War. With few
intermissions, the Fund has been represented every
year since 1920, generally in the closest collaboration
with its daughter institution, the British School of
Archæology in Jerusalem, whose successive directors,

John Garstang and J. W. Crowfoot, have also headed most of its expeditions. The first undertaking was the excavation of Ashkelon (Ascalon) in 1920–1.[75] Garstang and Phythian-Adams made some important discoveries bearing on the time of the Philistine occupation and the building activity of Herod the Great at Ascalon, but the site proved so difficult from the archæological point of view, that they were finally forced to give it up, for practical reasons. One difficulty with this site is that the Philistine stratum, in which scholars are naturally most interested, is covered with at least twenty-six feet (eight metres) of Hellenistic, Roman, and later remains.

Passing over some of the minor undertakings of the Fund and of the British School of Archæology, working independently,[76] we come to the resumption of its earlier work at Jerusalem. Warren and Bliss were now followed by Macalister, who returned to Palestine in 1923, after fourteen years' absence. With the help of a former assistant of Petrie, J. Garrow Duncan, Macalister began to excavate on the Ophel hill, just south of the Temple Area. In 1924, Duncan took sole charge of the work, which continued until 1925. Then, in 1927 and 1928, the excavation was continued under the direction of Crowfoot.[77] Jerusalem is a discouraging site in which to dig, because of the extraordinary vicissitudes which the city has undergone, vicissitudes which have either buried ancient remains under a mountain of débris, or have led to the complete removal of the débris of occupation, so that nothing is left the unfortunate archæologist when he digs down to what should be the proper level for important discoveries. As a matter of fact, Ophel was partly razed by Simon Maccabæus about 140 B. C., so

the excavator may expect to find little except in un-
disturbed caverns and pockets in the rock. When
Weill dug before and after the War at the southern
end of " Ophel," he found in situ only rock-cuttings,
which, however, tantalizingly included the lower parts
of several very ancient tombs of the so-called
Phœnician type, which may very well have belonged
to the series of royal tombs of the kings of Judah.[78]
Macalister, Duncan, and Crowfoot had the same disappointing experience until they reached the edge of
the hill on the eastern and western sides, where they
found extensive remains of the ancient city walls of
the Canaanite and Israelite periods. The wall of the
Israelite period (David and his successors) was found
to be eight metres (twenty-seven feet) wide on both
sides of the hill, a fact calculated to make us understand better how Jerusalem could offer such a long
and vigorous resistance to the Chaldæan arms in 588–7
B. C. The sloping revetment of the Israelite period
on the eastern slope of the hill is the most impressive
monument of Israelite fortification which we possess.[79]
The existence of so strong a wall on the western side,
east of the Tyropœon Valley, is an almost conclusive
proof of the correctness of the view originally proposed by Robertson Smith, and adopted independently
by Père Germer-Durand, that Pre-Maccabæan Jerusalem was restricted to the eastern hill, including
" Ophel " and the Temple Mount.[80] While this view
is not accepted by all scholars, the British excavations
have demonstrated to the satisfaction of the last " die-
hards " that the Jebusite and Davidic Zion, the oldest
Jerusalem, is " Ophel."

After the discovery of the Tomb of Tut-ankh-aman
had led to the adoption by the Egyptians of a very

narrow policy with regard to the share of antiquities which the excavator was given, the British School of Archæology in Egypt, founded and directed by Sir Flinders Petrie, decided to transfer most of its work to Palestine, especially the extreme south, where the closest contact with Egypt might, *a priori*, be expected. In 1927 Petrie began work at Tell Djemmeh, the site of ancient Biblical Gerar, which plays so important a rôle in the Patriarchal narratives of Genesis.[81] At Gerar he found work seriously impeded by the presence of many huge grain pits, or silos, built by the Persians in order to supply their army with grain, probably during an invasion of Egypt. After one campaign, in which he failed to get down beyond the Iron Age, except in a deep pit, he moved to Tell el-Fâr'ah, where he has conducted three campaigns (1928–30).[82] Tell el-Fâr'ah is situated southeast of Gaza, at the extreme southwest corner of the Israelite settlement. The identification of the site is uncertain, and Petrie's idea that it represents Beth-pelet of the Bible is quite without basis.[83] The most probable suggestion so far made is that Tell el-Fâr'ah is ancient Sharuhen, a point of strategic importance, mentioned a number of times in the Bible and the Egyptian inscriptions.[84]

The excavations around the base of the mound have yielded a very large number of tombs, belonging to the Middle and Late Bronze Ages, as well as to the various phases of the Iron Age. In the tombs, which thus cover nearly a millennium and a half, has been found an extraordinarily large quantity of pottery, of bronzes, scarabs, and jewelry. Historically, the most interesting objects are probably the scarabs, which have furnished Petrie with material to rearrange the relative chronology of Egyptian scarabs of the obscure period which intervened between the Twelfth and the Eighteenth Dynasties (about 1780–1570 B. C.), generally called the Hyksos Age. Petrie has found abundant evidence that Tell el-Fâr‘ah was an important Hyksos stronghold. A very remarkable system of fortification, consisting mainly of a very wide and deep moat, and showing clear affinities with the Hyksos fortification as we know it from Egypt and Syria,[85] was found to belong to the Hyksos Age. The latest discoveries on the mound have been of very great value for the reconstruction of life in Palestine in the Ramesside period, that is, about the time of the Conquest, or a little before. The Egyptian palace of this age, found a year ago, proved to be quite luxurious, containing such features as a bedroom with a raised recess for the bed, a bathroom connecting with it, and a wine storeroom.

This winter (1930–1) Petrie has begun excavations at the mound of Tell el-‘Addjûl, on the coast south of Gaza. The site is very large, covering several hundred acres, and seems to have been abandoned several hundred years before the Israelite occupation of the country. When so old a site is discovered, the excavator is able to penetrate at once into very early levels, and to elucidate little known periods of history, without having to spend months or years in digging laboriously and conscientiously through comparatively uninteresting post-Biblical levels, where it is seldom indeed that any really fresh material, of historical importance, comes to light. We may well look forward with interest to the continuation of excavations at Tell el-‘Addjûl, which is certain to yield much valuable information with regard to the relations between Egypt and Palestine in the third millennium, as well as in the following age of the Patriarchs.

In 1929 Garstang resumed work at Tell es-Sulṭân (Jericho), which the Germans had begun to excavate before the War (see above). Since he has just begun the second campaign (January, 1931), we must await its results before describing the work of the first campaign.[86] Suffice it to say that he has already obtained convincing proof that the German chronology of the fortifications was wrong, thanks to a very careful use of the pottery, in which he enjoys the help of such specialists as Vincent and Fisher. The most important problem which remains to be solved at Jericho is the exact date of the capture and destruction of the last Canaanite town on the site by the Israelites under Joshua. On the basis of the material published in the German account of the excavations before the War, different scholars have differed by two centuries or more in their date for this event. Only systematic excavation can solve this question, which is obviously of the greatest importance for Biblical chronology and history.

9. GERMAN AND DANISH EXCAVATIONS

Just before the War (1913–4) Sellin directed two very short campaigns at Tell Balâṭah, just outside modern Nâblus, in central Palestine. He correctly identified the site with the famous Biblical town of Shechem. As soon as possible, after the War, in 1926, he resumed excavation here, directing five campaigns, after which Dr. Welter-Mauve followed him with a sixth campaign (1928), making eight in all, short and long.[87] Unfortunately, owing to the employment by both Sellin and Welter of the trench system, it is not yet possible to form a clear idea of the stratification, or of the relation between the strata inside the walls and the city walls themselves. It is, however, clear that the Middle Bronze town (no trace has yet been found of a settlement before 2000 B. C.) was much smaller than the Late Bronze one, which was very extensive and important. A typical Hyksos fortress has been found under the remains of the later Canaanite and Israelite citadel, the Biblical Millo. Shortly afterwards, perhaps about 1600 B. C., though the date remains uncertain, for the reasons given above, the city was surrounded with a massive cyclopæan wall, the finest example of Canaanite masonry which we have in Palestine. The great size of the stones and the solidity of the masonry were required in order to ensure the safety of the city, located on a low eminence in the valley between Ebal and Gerizim. The two city-gates so far excavated, on the northwest and east, respectively, are also the most imposing gateways of the early period which have yet been found.

The most interesting discovery inside the city was a temple of the Late Canaanite period, in the Millo, and believed with reason to represent the temple of Baal-berith mentioned in the story of Abimelech, Jud. 8–9. This temple was found to have a rather complex history, covering most of the Late Bronze Age, and descending into the Early Iron. It would seem to have been destroyed by Abimelech, son of Gideon, about 1100 B. C. Very few tombs were discovered, since the excavation was restricted mainly to the interior of the town. Among small objects, the most important were some Israelite altars of incense and two Canaanite cuneiform tablets, both purely private documents, one a business contract, the other a letter.[88]

To what extent cuneiform must have been used by even ordinary Canaanites, especially in large towns, in the affairs of daily life is becoming increasingly evident. Such discoveries give us reason to hope that many more written documents from the age of the Patriarchs and the Conquest will yet be discovered in Palestine.

In 1926 and 1929 H. Kjaer and Aage Schmidt undertook the excavation of Seilûn, Biblical Shiloh, on behalf of a Danish committee.[89] The work here has been carried on slowly, with the most painstaking method which has yet been employed in Palestinian excavation. Since Shiloh was occupied down into the thirteenth century A. D., or even a little later, much time and patience are necessary before such conscientious excavators as the Danes can get down into Biblical levels. However, once such levels are reached, we may be sure that no scrap of evidence will be neglected, and that every possible care in recording will be taken. It is already certain that the settlement of the early Israelite age, when the Tabernacle stood at Shiloh, and pilgrimages were made to it by pious Israelites, was larger than at any subsequent period. The early Israelite occupation lasted apparently from the thirteenth to the eleventh centuries B. C., to judge from the pottery found. Most interesting is the fact that no remains have been discovered belonging to the period between the tenth and the sixth centuries, when, according to Biblical statements, Shiloh lay in ruins. We have, accordingly, archæological evidence, favouring the general view that Shiloh was destroyed by the Philistines after the battle of Ebenezer and the capture of the Ark (about 1050 B. C.). We may hope for the discovery of the site of the Tabernacle some day, since there is reason to believe that the tent of meeting was replaced by a stone building before the fall of Shiloh.[90]

10.   THE SYNAGOGUES OF GALILEE

While we are obliged to restrict ourselves in this lecture to the discoveries bearing more directly upon the Biblical period, we cannot entirely pass over the epoch-making researches which have been carried on since the War in two fields, one earlier and one later than Bible times.   Both have no little indirect interest and value for students of the Bible.   We refer primarily to the excavations of Jewish synagogues belonging to the Roman and Byzantine periods, and to the prehistoric researches which have been prosecuted with increasing energy since 1925.

The Jewish synagogues of Galilee have long attracted attention, and two German archæologists, H. Kohl and C. Watzinger, made a thorough examination of their surface remains, so far as they were known, with occasional soundings, some years before the War.[91]   The Franciscans, who had acquired the site of Capernaum, continued excavating the ruins of its synagogue until the latter was completely cleared and partly restored by Père Orfali, after the War.[92] The synagogue at Capernaum is by far the finest edifice of the kind which has yet been discovered in Palestine.   However, contrary to the opinion of the Franciscan fathers who own the site, it is agreed by all competent scholars, Catholic, Protestant and Jewish alike (since archæological and historical discussions are never affected seriously by confessional lines), that it was built between 150 and 250 A. D.[93]   Curiously enough, not a single surviving synagogue belongs to the New Testament period.   The reason for this apparent anomaly is naturally that most synagogues of Palestine were destroyed either in the first or the second Jewish revolt, that is, between 66 and 135 A. D. There is, however, reason to believe that the plan and disposition of the earlier synagogues was not very different from that of the synagogues of the Roman period, though the architecture and sculpture must have been of quite another type.

The two most important synagogues excavated since the War are, beyond doubt, those of Noaran ('Ain Dûq) near Jericho, cleared by Vincent in 1921,[94] and of Beth Alpha, near Beth-shan, excavated by Sukenik in 1929.[95] Both synagogues possessed elaborate mosaic floors, with inscriptions and pictorial representations. The structure at Noaran cannot be dated exactly, but belongs to the fourth or fifth centuries, while the other, dated in the reign of Emperor Justin, belongs to the early sixth century A. D. In 1929 a similar, though inferior synagogue, also from the fourth or fifth century, was discovered by Crowfoot at Gerasa (Djerash) in Transjordan.[96] At Noaran and at Beth Alpha elaborate representations of the twelve signs of the zodiac were found; at Noaran the figures had been destroyed by Jewish iconoclasts, who were opposed to pictorial imagery, but at Beth Alpha they were completely preserved. At the latter place there was even a representation of the sun, in human form, driving a four-horse chariot. Even more surprising is the fact that Biblical scenes were also represented on these synagogue mosaics. At Noaran there was a scene showing Daniel in the lions' den, at Beth Alpha the sacrifice of Isaac was depicted, while at Gerasa there was a mosaic representing Noah's ark and the animals. Dr. E. L. Sukenik, who is the foremost authority on the Jewish synagogues of Palestine, has been able to show that iconic decoration, far from being exceptional, was characteristic of the Roman and Byzantine periods, which correspond to the age of the Talmud. It was not until later that an intense iconoclastic reaction set in, especially in the west. From Sukenik's comparative studies we may safely expect important light on the evolution of the synagogue, as well as upon its origin in the Maccabæan age and its development in the last century of the Second Temple, which is also the time of Christ and the Apostles.[97]

11. PREHISTORIC ARCHÆOLOGY IN PALESTINE

Prehistoric research began in Palestine soon after the time of Robinson,[98] but until after the War it was limited to surface exploration and the collection of flint artifacts found above ground. A very little excavation had been undertaken by the Jesuit fathers, Père Zumoffen and others, in Phœnicia.[99] The results of this long continued, but mostly unsystematic surface study were gathered and published by Karge during the War.[100] While the types of flints were in the main correlated accurately with corresponding types found in Western Europe, there was no stratigraphical evidence to confirm the correlation, and no human skeletal remains had been discovered, so that nothing was known about the men who had lived then in the Holy Land. In 1925 a young English protoarchæologist, Turville-Petre, excavated two prehistoric caves in Galilee, between Magdala and Capernaum, just above the Sea of Galilee.[101] In one of them, Mughâret ez-Zuṭṭîyeh, he found a very clear stratification, with Mousterian (Middle Palæolithic) below and Aurignacian (Upper Palæolithic) above.

Most important, however, was a human skull and other skeletal remains of an absolutely clear Neanderthal type, found in the Mousterian level. Since many specimens of Neanderthal man have been found in Europe, and always, where there is stratigraphical evidence, in Mousterian levels, this discovery has definitively established the correlation between the Mousterian of Western Asia and that of Europe. Turville-Petre's brilliant discoveries have naturally spurred other prehistorians to participation in this work. In several campaigns Miss Dorothy Garrod, an eminent English proto-archæologist, has studied the prehistoric deposits in Palestinian caverns, especially at Shuqbah in southwestern Samaria and at Wâdî el-Mughârah south of Carmel.[102] In these caves she has made extremely important stratigraphical discoveries, showing a very complicated prehistory. Her most remarkable contribution has been the discovery and study of a new culture, belonging to the late Mesolithic, with African affinities, a culture which she has termed " Natufian." The people to whom this culture belonged were a Mediterranean race, of small stature and delicate form, and with a highly developed artistic sense. A figure of a young bull, carved from bone, is superior to any prehistoric art object yet found in Asia. The date of this culture is still, of course, doubtful, but cannot be later than the sixth millennium B. C. Père Mallon and M. René Neuville, chancellor of the French Consulate in Jerusalem, have also made some very important excavations in prehistoric sites. Under Neuville's direction, a cave in the Wâdî Khreiṭûn (the traditional site of Adullam, southeast of Bethlehem) has been excavated, and has proved to contain remains at least as old as the oldest found in French caves, that is, from the transition between Early and Middle Palæolithic.[103] Mallon and Neuville have more recently (1930) collaborated in the excavation of a neolithic (properly chalcolithic) village site just across the Jordan from Jericho, now called Tuleilât el-Ghassûl.[104] While the pottery and other remains are very primitive, they open up to the archæologist a whole new period of history, of which nothing was previously known. Since this is the period when grain was first cultivated, animals were first domesticated, and pottery was first made, it possesses an unusual interest for the student of the past. It is also very instructive to know that towns were already in existence in the Jordan Valley before 3000 B. C.[105]

In this lecture we have sketched the development of archæological research in Palestine, and have shown its gradual expansion, the increasing exactness of its methods. We have also shown how this improvement of technique leads to more and more important historical discoveries. Step by step, sometimes rapidly, sometimes slowly and cautiously, we advance the frontiers of our knowledge, filling up blank spaces on our chart, and enlarging our information concerning better known periods. Every detail will eventually find its place, and enable us better to reconstruct the historical background of the Bible. Because of its central position, discoveries in Palestine also possess very great value for the student of comparative civilization and world history. While we watch the progress of archæological discovery in Palestine we are also spectators at the unfolding of the greatest drama of history, the origin and early development of our own civilization and our own religion.[106]

II

UNEARTHING A BIBLICAL CITY

1. **THE INITIATION AND ORGANIZATION OF THE WORK
AT TELL BEIT MIRSIM**

IN April, 1924, the writer rode through the southern Shephelah of Judah with a small party of students of the American School of Oriental Research in Jerusalem. Among the mounds which we examined on that occasion was Tell Beit Mirsim. Approaching it as we did from the north, it impressed us greatly, both with its size and with its splendid situation. After we had ridden up to its southern side, from which the climb to the top is easy, we found that the revetment of the ancient walls was still exposed in part, and that the outlines of the piers of the main gateway, opening slightly south of east, were still visible. The surface of the mound was covered with Iron Age pottery, including numerous ring-burnished sherds of Early Iron II, but nothing of a later date. Bronze Age sherds also appeared on the slopes of the hill. The possibility that this was the site of the long-lost Debir, or Kiriath-sepher of the Bible immediately struck me, and after an examination of the other mounds of this region had yielded no serious competitor, the suggestion was published in the preliminary report of our trip.[1] On reading this report, Dr. M. G. Kyle, then president of Xenia

Theological Seminary in St. Louis, became interested
in the mound as a prospective site for excavation.
His offer to undertake a joint excavation here, under
his patronage and my direction, was accepted by the
Schools of Oriental Research, and the first campaign
was launched in the spring of 1926.

So far three joint campaigns, under the same auspices,[2] have been conducted at Tell Beit Mirsim, the
first from March to June, 1926,[3] the second from
April to June, 1928,[4] and the third from June to
August, 1930.[5] We hope to undertake a fourth campaign in the summer of 1932, *Deo volente*. While the
summer is somewhat warm, the site is so high (about
1600 feet above sea-level) that the weather is seldom
unpleasantly hot. In fact, during the third campaign
we slept under blankets nearly the whole time. Even
at noon, under canvas, it was rarely unbearably hot.
The southern Shephelah is so dry that malaria is
little known, so far as we could find. A great advantage of summer campaigns is that the harvest is over
before we begin digging, so there is no competition
and labour is cheap. Another advantage is that there
are either no crops at all, or simply such relatively
worthless summer crops as *dhurah*. It is, furthermore,
quite possible for scholars to come from America during their summer vacations, a fact which makes the
creation of an adequate staff much simpler.

The first campaign was organized on a very simple
basis. There were only five Americans on the regular
staff, not counting guests, who remained for a shorter
or a longer time.[6] The labourers, who averaged about
fifty in number, were divided into three small gangs,
each under the supervision of a member of the staff,
while a native foreman took charge of the lists of

workmen, and supervised the work during our absence. Some of my time was at first devoted to teaching the elements of Arabic to the members of the staff, who soon became so proficient that they could direct fluently, but became helpless as soon as the natives began replying.[7] On our second campaign we added an Egyptian surveyor, trained by Dr. C. S. Fisher, together with two Egyptian foremen, both obtained through Fisher.[8] This greatly eased my work, since I had to do most of the surveying and planning during the first campaign. Besides Kyle and myself, there were three other foreign members of the staff.[9] We averaged sixty to seventy labourers. The third campaign was organized on a much better basis, thanks to a considerable increase in the money available. There were seven foreign members of the staff, several of whom had previous experience, and all of whom worked with a whole-souled interest and loyalty which I have never seen surpassed.[10] We had three surveyors, all trained by Fisher,[11] and four native foremen, two of whom were Fisher's men. Four gangs, with an average total of about a hundred labourers, were employed. Another Egyptian devoted all his time to the mending of pottery, an art in which he had attained a very high degree of skill under Fisher's training. It is my conviction that we attempted to do more than was altogether prudent in our third campaign. When the director of an expedition can only spend three or four months in the country, more than half of which is spent in actual excavation, it is unwise, from the standpoint of scientific results, to employ more than an average of seventy men. It is much better to be content with few great discoveries and an adequate treatment of the material recovered than to make more discoveries at the expense of proper recording and study of what is found.

Our methods followed the principles worked out by Fisher, who, both as the first director of the major undertakings at Beth-shan and Megiddo, and as professor of archæology in the American Schools of Oriental Research (since 1925), has, as we emphasized in our first lecture, exercised a very great influence on the development of American archæological work in Palestine. Naturally, different sites and varying circumstances require varying application of his principles; he himself has been the first to change his methods in order to adapt them to conditions. The main points are: systematic and careful planning, surveying, and levelling; excavation of areas rather than trenches; full and exact drawing of pottery forms on millimetre-ruled paper; systematic recording and card-indexing, with the use of a large record-book for the detailed entry of all objects discovered. The main danger, in employing trained Egyptian or Palestinian foremen, is that the control exercised over them by the archæological staff may be inadequate. No matter how well trained these foremen may be, they can never attain more than a craftsman's technique; the purpose of the work eludes them, and they are nearly always helpless before new and complicated problems. Constant watchfulness is, accordingly, indispensable, and the director and his foreign assistants must always be ready to go to work with their own hands, or to spend entire days at a single point of interest. As soon as the organization becomes so elaborate that the director is no longer able to spend much of his time in the chantier of excavation, a small expedition ceases to have a scientific reason for existence, and should be replaced by one provided with a full-time organization, a permanent expedition house, and a professional staff. American organization tends to neglect direct control of the excavation itself; English and German organization shows a tendency to slight the recording in order to devote as much attention as possible to the chantier. To combine both methods is entirely possible for a small excavation with an adequate staff.

2. DEALING WITH THE ARABS: THE NATIVES OF THE DISTRICT

After this methodological excursus, let us return to the excavation of Tell Beit Mirsim! We have described the selection of the site and the organization of the expedition. The permit to excavate was granted each year anew by the Department of Antiquities, acting on the advice of the Archæological Advisory Board. It was then the duty of the director to negotiate with the native owners for lease of the site. Direct purchase of all or part of the site would naturally be more advantageous, and far less troublesome than lease, where the same wearying and sometimes intricate negotiations must be renewed before every campaign. Unfortunately, however, the mound of Tell Beit Mirsim is, like so much property in Palestine, meshâ' land, that is, it is owned in common by a large number of different families and persons, most of whom belong to a single clan, the 'Arâqbîyeh,[12] which resides during most of the year in neighbouring ruins, or khirab. There were two groups of members of this clan which had to be considered, with three representatives. The minor members seldom offered much opposition to an agreement which their head-men, acting as agents, had concluded, though they were much given to intriguing before the agents had acted. " Double-crossing " is familiar in virtually all Arab business transactions; honesty, as we understand it, is all but non-existent. However, I have seldom known an Arab to break his word after it is once given, and oral transactions or agreements are still much more common than written ones. An added complication—or simplification, as the case may be— in dealing with the people of this district is that their main ancestral stock is only ten generations from the desert, and they are, consequently, very much under the influence of the chief sheikhs of the community. Before explaining this situation, a word with regard to the latter is necessary.

Tell Beit Mirsim lies opposite Khirbet Beit Mirsim, a Byzantine ruin which is now, like most other ruins in this region, occupied during most of the year by peasants, who live in caves, tents, or booths among the ruins. The capital of the community is the town of Dûrā, ancient Adora, Biblical Adoraim, which lies up in the hills southwest of Hebron.[18] The people of Dûrā number officially over six thousand, but claim a population of ten thousand; their mode of life makes an accurate census quite impossible. During practically the entire year they live in their " ninety-nine khirab (ruins)," though the government reduces this round number to the more modest one of fifty-odd. They are divided into four groups of clans, each one under a chief, or mukhtâr. Yûsif 'Abd el-Ḥamîd, mukhtâr of the area in which Tell Beit Mirsim lies, is the grandson of the redoubtable 'Abd er-Raḥmân, chief of Dûrā, and overlord of all the Hebron and Beersheba region, as far as the Egyptian frontier, a century ago.[14] 'Abd er-Raḥmân was deposed by the Turks, when they regained their power in Palestine, about 1839, and later exiled to Cyprus, where he died. Most of our dealings have been, perforce, with Yûsif, who is both an Arab gentleman and a clever man, as we have had ample occasion both to applaud and to regret.

One of the most interesting recreations of my first campaign at Tell Beit Mirsim was to collect the historical traditions of Dûrā from intelligent natives, so far as possible of different families. Ten generations ago, that is, about the middle of the seventeenth century, when the power of the Turkish Government was weak, and the Syrian province was being devastated by the conflicts between the parties of Qeis and Yemen,[15] Dûrā was inhabited by peasants of older vintage, whose ancestors had probably come in from the desert two or three centuries earlier, though the modern occupants naturally know nothing about the history of their predecessors. To the neighbourhood of Dûrā came an Arab clan from the region of Ṭafîleh in what was once the land of Edom. This clan, the Abū Darâhimeh,[16] was an offshoot of the great Ḥedjâz tribe of the Benī Rabî‘,[17] which had migrated northward from the region of the Holy Cities of Islam some generations previously. The Abū Darâhimeh soon entered into marriage relations with a clan (ḥamûleh) of Dûrā, whose clients they became. Not long afterwards, a girl from the Arab camp entered the town in order to grind some meal, but was seized and deflowered by a youth of the town. Being too weak to demand satisfaction, the Abū Darâhimeh bided their time, and plotted with the friendly clan of Dûrā to wreak revenge on the rest of the townsmen.

Some time later the chance presented itself; the Arabs offered a feast to the notables of the town, who came unarmed, while all the Arabs and their allies concealed daggers under their robes. At a prearranged signal, the hosts leaped to their feet and massacred the guests —a breach of the laws of Arab hospitality which could only be excused by the exigencies of the case. Meanwhile, other Arabs had concealed themselves, heavily armed, in a thicket near the threshing-floors where many of the men of Dûrā were at the time engaged in peaceful labour. An old man was sent down the road which ran by the threshing-floors toward the ambush; he drove an ass laden with *faqûs* (a kind of melon). When he approached the ambush he spilled the melons, and at this signal, also prearranged, several Arabs leaped out on him, while he cried for help. The threshers rushed to his assistance, and were promptly set upon and massacred by the concealed Arabs. We have no space to describe subsequent happenings, nor to recount the wars which Dûrā fought during the eighteenth and early nineteenth century, extraordinarily interesting though the narrative is, compounded equally of history and folklore. The striking resemblance of the story which we have told with certain narratives of the Bible is evident [18]; as given me by the natives, the similarity is even greater, since the account is interlarded with ætiological observations, connecting the names of places around Dûrā with events in its history—sometimes, no doubt, correctly, but often quite fancifully.[19]

3. HISTORICAL SKETCH OF THE EXCAVATION

In our first campaign we began by clearing the East Gate, removing the débris without disturbing any

of the masonry, which still stands. While this method
made it difficult to give plans of the lower constructions, below the top level, we felt that the gateway
was too interesting to be destroyed. As the Arabs
have damaged it seriously since it was first cleared,
we expect to excavate it completely in a later campaign. We then turned our attention to the West
Gate, which was also cleared in the same way, and
still stands, uninjured. In the Iron Age, these two
gates were the only modes of ingress into the city.
The East Gate, which opens out into a pre-exilic road
running southeast into the hill-country, and still in
part preserved, is wide enough for chariots, while the
West Gate, which led to a very ancient road running
north and south along the Wâd el-Bayyârah, is narrow, only admitting pedestrians and laden asses. Both
gates are solidly built, and exhibit the same indirect
method of entrance which is found to-day in Eastern
city gates, as in the Damascus Gate at Jerusalem.
Together they form the best examples of Early Iron
gateways which have yet been discovered in Palestine.

We further cleared nearly the entire line of the city
wall of the Iron Age, leaving only a short sector in
the northwest, which is almost entirely destroyed, and
very deeply buried. Inside the town we limited ourselves to work in the top stratum. Just north of the
West Gate we cleared a large tower, of extremely
good Iron Age construction. The tower consisted of
a fairly large open court in the center, with rooms
opening from it in three directions, and abutting directly on the gateway and the city wall. That this
tower building was employed for public affairs is
indicated by a number of standard weights which we
found there; the best is a perfect eight mina weight

of polished limestone.[20]   It goes without saying that
one of the principal duties of the magistrates was to
adjudicate cases of disputed weights and measures.
In order to settle some difficult questions regarding the
age of the substructure of the West Gate, we dug
down to bed-rock just to the north of it, inside one
of the tower rooms. We soon found that we were in
a narrow rock-cut tunnel, leading down and into the
city, filled with débris containing exclusively Middle
Bronze pottery. Judge our disappointment when, instead of emerging into an untouched necropolis of the
time of the Patriarchs, we broke into a great empty
cistern, or rather group of cisterns, belonging to the
Iron Age! The Israelites, in digging a cistern, had
broken into the Canaanite sepulchral caverns, which
they had cleared, plastered, and used as a cistern—
another illustration of the facts underlying the double
use of the word *bor* in Hebrew, in the sense of " cistern " and of " Sheol."

North of the East Gate we cleared an area just
inside the city wall, with houses of the top stratum.
Curiously enough, the exigencies of space forced the
Israelites to tear out the inside of the city wall here,
in order to make room for their own dwellings, so
that the wall was nothing but a shell at this point.
While engaged in clearing the outside of the wall,
down to bed-rock, in this sector, we met with a second
disappointment. A cleft in the rock was found by the
labourers, who were ordered to widen it with their
picks, since there seemed to be a cave behind it. When
the entrance hole was large enough, we entered, together with a number of greatly excited Arabs. As we
crawled on and on, through apparently labyrinthine
passages, dimly lighted by tallow candles, the Arabs

became more and more intoxicated with the hope of finding buried treasure. Finally, one of them began, in his madness, to tell the others, in our hearing, what they must do when they had discovered the gold— cut the throats of the *khawādjât,* and escape with the treasure. I was not at all disturbed by this sanguinary threat, which my companions failed to understand, since it had already become evident that the place had been used for nothing more romantic than storage bins for grain and straw, oil, etc. The Arabs were bitterly disappointed, and slunk out muttering, *mesākîn, bâqū fellāḥîn zeiyna,* " Poor people, they were peasants like us." The noisiest of the party disappeared for several weeks, apprehending ill-will on our part. As a matter of fact, he has never been allowed to forget that episode, which he recalls silently, with a sheepish grin.

When we cleared this group of caverns later, we obtained conclusive evidence that they had originally served as sepulchral chambers, which were entered through a doorway of typical Bronze Age megalithic construction, from the interior of the town. In the cave we discovered some interesting potsherds and other objects, all of which had fallen through clefts in the rock from above. This second disappointment has effectually discouraged our search for tombs. That the tombs of the ancient inhabitants were under the town rather than in the surrounding hills is evident both from these experiences of ours, and from the fact that the natives are entirely ignorant of the existence of any tombs in the hills. Since a successful search for tombs at the base of the hill on which our mound rises would infallibly lead to wholesale despoliation by the Arabs after our departure, as has happened, *e. g.*, at Gezer, we are slow about attempting it.

In the northwest quadrant of the mound we had noticed in 1924 that a group of large, and apparently rounded stone pillars projected from the surface of the ground. This group of pillars we not unnaturally took to be a "high-place." On excavating it, in our first campaign, it proved to be purely profane, and to consist of several groups of four stone pillars each of which served to support the ceiling of ancient Israelite houses. In extending our excavation here, we found the first of our dye-plants, which we also first regarded as a cult installation, though its true purpose rapidly dawned on us. We shall discuss these installations below.

Just inside the East Gate we correctly assumed that there would be an open space, unoccupied by houses, so we sank two shafts to bed-rock, which we reached in a little more than four metres. The first shaft, which served as a guide, was only two metres square, and we cleared it in half-metre stages, so as to secure a pottery index to the stratification. Just beside it, we then dug a second shaft, four metres square, which we dug according to the stratigraphic indications of the first pit, thus paralleling the arbitrary division of sherds by another division which followed the burned levels, so far as possible. In digging at the two gateways, we had already discovered the layers of ashes that form so characteristic a feature of our excavation. Since we had found four superimposed periods of construction at the East Gate with another older layer of débris, we tentatively inferred the existence of four strata, which corresponded, respectively, to our present G—F, E—C (with two phases), B, and A. Our rough chronology for these four periods was based on the pottery, and was quite correct.

It was disappointing not to find any inscriptions or even stamped jar handles. But, all in all, we were satisfied with the results of the first campaign, and planned a second campaign two years later, in order to begin the stratigraphical study of the interior of the town. In this season we devoted our principal attention to an extensive area just to the south of the East Gate, along the inside of the city wall. After clearing the top stratum over this area, and discovering three more dye-plants, precisely like the one unearthed in the first campaign, we marked off a somewhat smaller area, and excavated three additional strata, B, C, and D, extending from the seventeenth to the tenth century B. C. Our most remarkable find was made at the very end of the campaign, when we began to clear a large and well-built house of the D stratum, and discovered a broken and partly calcined stela representing the serpent-goddess in relief. We also extended the excavation of the A level in the northwest quadrant to the south, but without making any remarkable discoveries. In the second campaign, besides gathering a mass of material bearing on the history and life of the town in different periods of its existence, we were successful in finding a few small inscriptions, both stamped jar handles and characters incised on vases before they were broken. Most interesting was the seal of Eliakim, servant of Joiachin, which will be discussed below.

The third campaign, in the summer of 1930, was, as we have already stated, the most elaborately organized of all, and more débris was, consequently, moved than in either of the previous campaigns. Our

first task was to continue excavating the area southwest of the East Gate, which we had cleared as far
down as stratum D in the second campaign. We had
then inferred the existence of two additional levels,
which we called provisionally " E " and " F," making
six in all. However, as we dug down, level by level,
in this area, new layers of ashes, covering new foundations of walls, followed one another, until we had
found five new strata, E—I, all belonging to the Middle Bronze, after which we reached the Early Bronze
level, which we termed J. Our work in this area thus
established the existence on the site of no fewer than
ten quite distinct strata. At the same time that this
work was going on, we began excavating a still larger
area, of about 2000 square metres, immediately to the
southwest, along the inside of the city wall. Here
we cleared the upper three strata, A—C, and began
the excavation of D in the " palace " area, where the
stela of the serpent-goddess had been found. This
large house was entirely cleared, and a unique set of
playing pieces, with a teetotum, was found; we shall
describe it below. Our most remarkable finds were
made in stratum C, near the end of the campaign. We
were able to show, while clearing C, that there had
been a more or less continuous destruction and conflagration in the middle of the period, so that we must
distinguish two periods, designated as C_1 and C_2.
There are in all, therefore, no less than eleven layers
of débris on our site, all separated from the adjacent
ones by burned levels. If J proves to be composite, as
it very likely will, we may have even more. It was
in C_2 that we found the Canaanite table of offerings,
with three lions in relief around the rim, and on the
very last day of excavation a unique stone lion.

In the third campaign we greatly extended our knowledge regarding the detailed chronology of the site, both in confirmation and in further development of the results secured in our second campaign. Thus, for instance, we established the chronology of the Late Canaanite period, stratum C. We also confirmed the division of stratum B, the first Israelite occupation level, into three phases, pre-Philistine, Philistine, and post-Philistine, the value of which for Biblical history is evident. Further confirmation was secured for our previous ascription of the destruction of B to Shishak. Finally, we succeeded in differentiating more exactly between the successive phases of A, and especially in proving conclusively that the latest Jewish town on the site was destroyed by the Chaldæans at the time of the last invasion of Judah, in 588–7 B. C. All these points will be discussed below.

4. THE IDENTIFICATION OF THE ANCIENT CITY

After this sketch of the history of our excavation, let us turn to the history of the ancient town and its culture in successive ages, as revealed by the pick and hoe, and interpreted by comparative archæological methods. At the beginning of this lecture it was stated that we had provisionally identified the site with Biblical Debir or Kiriath-sepher. This identification is not certain, since no inscriptions bearing the name were found in the first three campaigns. We regard it ourselves as practically certain, though we do not care to stress this personal conviction because of the inability of other scholars to control some of our arguments. Our first argument is based on the familiar topographical method of elimination, which has been decisive in the case of innumerable other ancient

places.   Kiriath-sepher was the most important of
a group of eleven towns which are listed in Joshua
15 as being in the sixth district of Judah.[21]   So far
as the other ancient names have been preserved in
modern times, these towns are all, aside from a mis-
placed group of three towns at the end of the list,
situated in the extreme southwestern part of the hill-
country, where the mountains (*ha-Har*), the low hill-
country (*hash-Shefelah*), and the dry plains to the
south (*han-Negeb*) meet.[22]   Judging from the collo-
cation of names, it has long been the fashion for Biblical topographers, who have only been influenced by
archæological evidence in the most recent years, to
identify Debir with modern eẓ-Ẓâherîyeh, pronounced
eḍ-Ḍâherîyeh by the city Arabs.[23]   Since this name has
a perfectly good Arab etymology, and, moreover, has
only one letter in common with Hebrew *Debîr,* the
identification is ludicrous from the linguistic point of
view.   The site shows no remains older than the Roman period, and lacks the ground-water which was
essential to the life of a Canaanite city.   The combination is, therefore, exceedingly bad.   Now let us
consider other possibilities.   First of all, we must
search for a mound, since Kiriath-sepher was a
Canaanite royal city, after which it was the residence
of Othniel, first judge of Israel, continuing to be inhabited down into a comparatively late pre-exilic
period, as we know from the fact that it figures in
the lists of Jewish towns of the monarchy (Jos. 15).
Having been a walled town at several different periods, the chances that it is not represented by a large
mound are extremely slender.   The only mounds in
the district where Kiriath-sepher was located, and
which have not otherwise been identified are Tell

Beit Mirsim, Tell el-Khuweilifeh, and Tell ʿAiṭûn, the
latter two being south and north of the former, respectively. The mound of Tell el-Khuweilifeh [24] exhibits, to judge from surface indications, a history
very much like that of Tell Beit Mirsim, but it is
considerably smaller. However, its location throws
it definitively into the Negeb of Simeon, and consequently quite outside of the sixth district of Judah.
There can be little doubt that Khirbet Umm er-
Ramāmîn, just to the south of it, in the same physical
environment, represents the Rimmon of Simeon.[25]
Tell ʿAiṭûn does not exhibit any traces of Bronze Age
occupation at all, and, therefore, drops out of consideration for our purpose.[26] It may be added that
Jos. 10:38, which says that Joshua went up directly
from Eglon to Hebron, from which he returned to
Debir, also proves a location of the latter south of
the direct line of march from Tell el-Ḥesî [27] to Hebron
—south since all the definitely located towns of the
sixth district of Judah, where Debir lay, are much to
the south of this line. Furthermore, Jos. 11:21 suggests a location between Hebron and Anab, in remarkable agreement with the actual situation of our site.
The modern name, Tell Beit Mirsim, is derived, as is
very often the case in Palestine, from the adjacent
Byzantine ruin of Khirbet Beit Mirsim. As might be
expected, the latter bears an Aramaic name, probably
standing for *Beth-barsama* or *Beth-barsima* [28]; *mursim*
(whence *mirsim*) is an Arabic popular etymology,
meaning " a man who makes a camel walk fast."

The most decisive argument for the identification is
now derived from the archæological history of our
mound, which shows a most perfect parallelism with
the documentary history of Kiriath-sepher. The name,

which meant originally "scribe-town," not "book-town," is characteristic of the Bronze Age, though the town is not, apparently, mentioned in cuneiform or Egyptian sources.[29] The absence of such mention does not prove anything, since few of the towns of southern Palestine are mentioned in our external sources, owing to the fact that this part of the country seldom joined in the revolts against Egyptian suzerainty. Hebrew tradition, correct in other similar cases, makes it one of the Canaanite "royal cities," that is, residences of feudal barons of that age. Our excavations have shown that the town was most important in the Middle and Late Bronze Ages, and was undoubtedly the residence of a baron (*awilu*).[30] It was destroyed most completely, the fortifications being completely demolished, and the town burned, in a conflagration so intense that in some places there is a layer of ashes three feet thick. Immediately after this destruction a new town was built, so shortly afterwards that the foundation stones of the city wall and of the houses were in part laid in the ashes of the preceding destruction. Yet there was a very complete transformation in the character of the culture, so complete that we can only explain it by the settlement of a different people. It is obvious that this situation well illustrates the story of the capture of the town by Othniel ("Joshua"),[31] who burned it, and later made it his residence, from which he exercised the vague influence of a *shôpheṭ* ("judge"). Our site continued to be occupied down to the Babylonian exile, sharing a destruction at the hands of the barbarian mercenaries of Shishak with many other towns of Judah. After its destruction by the Chaldæans in 588–7 B. C., it was never occupied again, and even the name was forgotten and replaced by a new Aramaic one in the Roman period. The same is true of Debir, which is never mentioned in post-exilic or later sources.[32] Our identification, while not, accordingly, quite certain, is of the same order of probability as that of Gerar with Tell Djemmeh.[33] It cannot be compared with such certain identifications as that of Tell el-Mutesellim with Megiddo or of Tell el-Fûl with Gibeah of Saul, but it is very much better than that of Tell el-Ḥesī with Lachish,[34] of Tell eṣ-Ṣâfī with Gath,[35] or of Tell el-Fârʿah with Beth-pelet.[36] The case of Tell en-Naṣbeh, which is either Mizpah or Ataroth, is different, and can hardly be compared with any other topographical problem, because of the division of authorities.[37]

5. THE CULTURAL HISTORY OF THE EARLIEST STRATA (J—F)

If we transport ourselves back to about 2200 B. C., we find ourselves in a very different country from the southern Shephelah of our own day. Archæological excavations have proved conclusively that the hills of the western slope of Judah were then rather heavily wooded, though the timber was mostly of the type known as " scrub." [38] But the hand of man was already at work levelling the forests, and the hill on which the new town was first built by the Amorites [39] had already been cleared of its trees and washed bare by the winter rains before the town was standing long enough to accumulate débris of its own. We accordingly find the débris of occupation lying directly on bed-rock; it is only in pockets in the rock that the original red soil remains under the black soil containing human artifacts. Our town belonged to a number founded in the same general period in the hill-country; the coastal plains and the Jordan Valley had long since been dotted with towns, some of which were founded far back in the chalcolithic, perhaps more than a thousand years before the first continuous occupation of Tell Beit Mirsim.[40] Between the sparsely scattered towns there wandered semi-nomadic tribes, just as did the Hebrews in the Patriarchal Age. We have as yet recovered nothing but broken pottery from this level; the sherds belong to the latter part of the Early Bronze, being later, on the whole, than the bulk of the pottery from such typical Early Bronze settlements as Bâb ed-Drâ' in the Dead Sea valley,[41] and Tell el-Ḥesī I, down on the edge of the Philistine plain.[42] Our estimate for the duration of this first period of the life of our town, which, incidentally, may itself include more than one destruction and reoccupation, is purely arbitrary; we have no means of knowing whether it lasted a century, or two centuries, or even longer.

We have already stated that periods I—D, six strata, are all from the Middle Bronze, extending back from the first half of the sixteenth century, when D was destroyed, to about 2000 B. C. This date is also somewhat arbitrary, but cannot be moved more than a century in either direction. Our first two levels, I and H, are very similar to one another, and represent the transition from Early to Middle Bronze. Egyptian Middle Empire types of pottery begin to appear, interspersed with survivals from the Early Bronze of Canaan. Incised decoration, with straight lines, wavy lines, and notches,[43] becomes very common; black, pattern punctured, pear-shaped (piriform) juglets,[44] with double handle and button base, make their début. A characteristic type of vessel, which first comes in at this time, and lasts for several centuries, is a somewhat squat, cylindrical cooking pot, with flat bottom, made of very coarse ware; below its rim runs a raised band with thumb imprints, above which are a series of holes punctured through the vessel, originally intended, it would appear, to let out the steam while food was cooking in the pot. I—H may be dated somewhere in the twentieth and nineteenth centuries B. C. The fortifications of this age have not yet been discovered, and very little except pottery has been found to illustrate the life of the people.

With G we come to a better preserved stratum, and begin to get a clearer picture of the culture of the period. The city wall of G has been excavated for a considerable distance, and seems to extend most of the way around the hill, though in places it has been completely destroyed. At the points where it has appeared, its width is 3.25 metres, or eleven feet, but it is built of comparatively small stones, and no trace of a revetment has yet been found. It bears no resemblance either to the massive revetment walls of the Hyksos age, or to the still more massive cyclopæan walls of such Middle Bronze sites as Qurûn Ḥaṭṭîn (Madon), Tell Djâbiyeh, Irbid, or Tell esh-Shihâb, the first being in Galilee, the others in Eastern Palestine.[45] In G we excavated the entire enclosed courtyard of a large house, the rest of which remains to be examined in another campaign. This is the first appearance of a house plan which seems to survive in the "palace" of the E—D period (for which see below). Both are characterized by having a large rectangular walled court, three sides of which are exterior, while the fourth (opposite the entrance from the street) gives access, through two doors, to the ground floor of the house proper. The outside entrance of the G house was well preserved, and, to judge from the large stone door socket, was furnished with a solid wooden door. After the Middle Bronze Age this type of house disappears completely; nothing could be less characteristic of the houses of the Israelite period. In B—A for instance, the court, with its outside door, is either entirely absent, or is very differently planned; the houses themselves do not have the remotest similarity. In the court of this G house we were able to prove that there had been two successive phases of construction, in the second of which the level of the floor was actually lowered some 25 cm. One door was then closed, and three round constructions of stone and mortar, apparently for the purpose of holding storejars, were built lengthwise of the court. This court was obviously not intended for horses, as seems to have been the case with the Hyksos house, with which we have found such striking similarities of plan. As a matter of fact, we know from other sources that horses and horse-drawn chariots had not yet been introduced into Palestine and Egypt.

The pottery of our G level was both abundant and diversified. A comparison of it with the pottery found by Macalister in his tomb 28 II of Gezer, belonging to the royal necropolis,[46] showed such striking points of resemblance that I at once assigned it to about the same period, that is, to the early eighteenth century, with ample margin on either side (i. e., 1850–1750). The Gezer tomb can be dated to the Thirteenth Dynasty in Egypt by its scarabs. I then asked the two most eminent authorities on the pottery of Palestine, Père Vincent and Dr. C. S. Fisher, to give absolutely independent judgments of the date of the pottery, which they courteously consented to do, though without our advantage of employing the stratification of the tell as a guide and check. Vincent assigned it, after careful examination, to about the nineteenth century B. C., while Fisher thought that it was older than about 1800 B. C., but not very much earlier. And yet there are scholars who fancy that the chronology of Palestinian pottery is still as obscure as it was before the War! Few small objects, aside from pottery, have yet been found in level G. The most interesting object was a broken limestone mould for casting bronze axe-heads and lance-heads.

The F level shows a continuation of the G culture, with the use of the same fortifications, though the preceding city had been destroyed by fire, and the houses of the new settlement were built on entirely new foundations. We must evidently date F somewhere in the eighteenth century B. C.

6. THE STRATA OF THE HYKSOS AGE (E—D)

With the E stratum there is an abrupt change in the history of the town. The E level itself is rather thin, and the next occupation, of the D period, shows restoration on the same foundations, together with the addition of many poorer houses, built in space which had been left open in E. For practical purposes, therefore, we may consider the E—D levels as representing a single historical period. From numerous scarabs, nearly all of which were discovered in houses of D, we know that E—D belong to the Hyksos period in the narrow sense, *i. e.,* to the age of the great barbarian irruption and of the feudal empire which was erected by the barbarians, with a focus in the Egyptian Delta. The fortification which was erected by the E people, and which continued in use, with various changes and restorations, down to the end of the Canaanite occupation (C_2), was essentially the same as that of the so-called red city of Jericho, and dates from the same time, about 1700 B. C. The city wall was of stone below and adobe brick above, while the stone substructure generally sloped outward, forming a revetment as well as a substructure for the brick wall. In some places there was also a retaining wall, but it would appear that the retaining wall represents a secondary feature of Late Bronze Age, in most cases, at least. This question can only be settled after more extensive excavations of the Bronze Age wall remains.

In the southeast quadrant, inside the city wall, we found that the D stratum is remarkably well preserved. Here, in square SE 22, we cleared a large, well-built house, which we dignified by the term " palace." As stated above, the house is built on E foundations. Entrance to the house from the front was through a large court, containing a round, plastered trough, evidently used for feeding animals. The gate was wide enough, it would seem, to admit a chariot, so we seem to be justified in supposing that the court and the rooms on the ground floor were used in part to furnish quarters for a chariot and horses. There were five rooms on the ground floor, together with a small back court, with a rear egress. The walls were about four feet thick, of adobe on stone foundations; they were well plastered with white lime plaster. The members of the household lived in the upper two stories; that there were two upper stories may be inferred both from house models found at Beth-shan and elsewhere, and from the abnormal thickness of the walls of the first story. Two of the five rooms in the first floor served as storerooms, and were full of more or less broken store-jars when found—between twenty and thirty, which originally contained wine and oil. One room was entered by a flight of two steps rising to a somewhat higher elevation, with a narrow bench on one side of the room; it may have served as an anteroom, since the staircase leading to the upper story apparently started at one end of it, though no trace of it was left. The other two rooms, connected by a wide arch, opened separately on the front court, and in view of their disposition and the total absence of any indication that they had been used either for stores or for living quarters, may safely be supposed to have been employed as stables for horses.

Inside this house were discovered a number of unique objects, which had fallen into the rooms of the first floor at the time of the destruction of the city by fire, either from the second or the third story. Nearly a metre above the floor of the first room excavated, a magazine for wine or oil, we found a calcined stela, with the upper part missing, and the original surface reduced to lime-dust by the violence of the conflagration. The stela was originally about a foot wide by two feet high (now 30 by 42 cm.), and was clearly inserted into a niche in the wall, since the front, bearing a representation of the serpent-goddess in relief, is flat, while the back is rounded cylindrically, and the flat base still has cement plaster adhering to it. We may safely suppose, since the house was unquestionably a private residence, that one of the up-

stairs rooms was fitted up as a kind of oratory. This
is the first representation of the serpent-goddess to be
found in Palestine, and is also unique as an illustration of the appearance of Canaanite idols.[47]   Since its
discovery two other representations of the Canaanite
serpent-goddess have been found, one by Grant at
Beth-shemesh; the other by Miss Garrod in a cave
near 'Athlît.[48]   The divinity of Tell Beit Mirsim appears as a draped figure, wearing a long robe, reaching
to the ankles.   The waist and one elbow are also
preserved, but the entire upper part of the figure is
lost, so that we are left in entire ignorance of her
head-dress, one of the most characteristic features of
an ancient Oriental deity.   Fortunately, the serpent
is completely preserved; it is a large snake, probably
a python, which comes out of the earth between her
ankles, coils around her legs, while its head is seen
between her thighs.   In Grant's Astarte plaque we
have a typical Qadesh (see below), with both arms
upraised, holding long-stemmed flowers, while a serpent crawls down over her naked body from her left
shoulder, its head reaching her left hip.[49]   Miss Garrod
discovered a (still unpublished) clay statuette of the
Hellenistic period, considerably larger than the figurines of the early period.   The goddess is shown
naked, with a serpent crawling up her right thigh.
It will be noticed that in all these cases the serpent's
head is directed toward the vulva of the goddess,[50] a
fact which proves conclusively that the serpent represents primarily the fecundizing *vis naturæ,* while the
fertilized goddess brings forth vegetation, symbolized
by the flowers which she holds.   In certain cases the
figure of Qadesh is shown holding one or two serpents
aloft, a curious conflation of two originally distinct

motives.[51]   Serpent-goddesses were common in the
ancient Orient; in Egypt we have, *inter alias,* the
harvest goddess Renen-wetet, while in Babylonia various serpent-goddesses were worshipped from the
earliest times.[52] The same is also true of Asia Minor
and the Ægean.[53]

At the opposite end of the house was found a unique
set of playing pieces, including five little blue faience
cones, five little blue faience three-cornered pyramids,
and an ivory teetotum.[54] The cones are one of the
commonest types of Egyptian playing pieces, but the
pyramids are unique. We had previously found an
exactly identical pyramid in another house of stratum
D. Enquiry among the leading European Egyptologists failed to throw light on the subject, until the
late Dr. Hall of the British Museum was consulted.
He knew of two or three similar objects in the British
Museum, but had always considered them as amulets
of some sort. The specimens in the British Museum
are all of the Saite period, a thousand years or more
after the date of the Tell Beit Mirsim pyramids. The
ivory teetotum appears to be unknown to Egyptian
archæologists, though the truncated pyramid was one
of the most familiar geometric forms in ancient
Egypt. The next oldest specimen is apparently Greek,
after which the teetotum was revived in modern times.
It is very curious to find that such important light on
early Egyptian games should come from Palestine.
On each of the four sides of the teetotum are round
holes, from one to four in number. The object was
twirled in the hand, and thrown like a die, the moves
of the game being dependent upon the number of
holes on the side which fell uppermost. There is very
good reason to believe that the game was played on

a board of twenty squares, specimens of which have
been found in Egypt (Middle and Late Empire) and
Assyria (late period).[55]

In the large house, as well as in the poorer houses
between it and the city wall, which were apparently
the homes of humbler folk, were found a number of
steatite and paste scarabs, all of characteristically
Hyksos type. The pottery was throughout of the
type to be expected in the transition from Middle to
Late Bronze. For example, the pear-shaped perfume
juglets known as Tell el-Yahūdiyeh vases, generally
black, with simple geometric patterns in punctured,
white-filled ornament, with a pointed button base and
a double handle, common through the strata H—E,
now become scarce, though they still occur. Since
they are common in all settlements of the Hyksos
period, their nearly complete absence in D shows that
we have reached the very end of the Middle Bronze.
The thin, hard-baked pottery of Cypro-Phœnician
type, generally known as base-ring ware, begins to appear in D, but the wishbone-handled bowl with gray or
cream slip and "ladder" patterns is entirely absent.
Both types are ubiquitous in C, as well as in all other
Palestinian sites of the Late Bronze Age. In general,
all the ordinary types of the Middle Bronze still occur
in our D stratum, but have all disappeared before the
level of Tuthmosis III (first half of fifteenth century
B. C.) at Beth-shan. The pottery from this period
at Beth-shan, my knowledge of which I owe to the
generosity of Mr. Rowe, is absolutely identical with
our C_1 ware. It is, therefore, quite certain that our
D level represents a culture which ceased to exist
before the fifteenth century. Since we have been able
to establish the fact that there was a period after the

fall of D in which the site was not occupied, it follows
that we are justified in connecting the destruction of
D with the events which accompanied the Egyptian
conquest of southern Palestine, after the expulsion
of the Hyksos. The Hyksos were driven out of Egypt
during the reign of Amosis I (cir. 1580–55 B. C.), and
the invasion of Palestine took place very soon afterwards, in the same reign. We may provisionally date
the fall of Tell Beit Mirsim about 1560–1550 B. C.,
but this date must not be regarded as definitive; a
date in the sixteenth century is, however, certain. The
destruction of the D city was exceedingly complete,
and was accompanied by a terrific conflagration. No
clear trace of looting was found, the contents of the
houses perishing with the inhabitants in the same destruction. Numerous remains of inlaid furniture and
boxes, especially in the palace, bore mute witness to
the suddenness of the catastrophe. Traces of a bitter
struggle could be followed in skeletons and weapons.
The remains of skeletons found—all in an extremely
friable condition—represented elderly persons and
children, as well as apparently bodies of men of fight-
ing age, lying prone on the ground where they had
been killed.[56] Among the weapons were bronze lance-
heads and daggers, a stone and a bronze mace-head,
etc.

7. THE LATE BRONZE AGE (C)

Some years—possibly decades—after the fall of D,
the site was reoccupied by new inhabitants, who
founded a new town, after they had levelled the ruins
of the preceding city. The same line of revetment
was employed, but the new settlers were not satisfied
with the strength of the old method of construction,

in which the wall was built on the revetment. They accordingly built a new wall rising just behind the revetment, and serving as a retaining wall for the upper part of it. Where this wall has been certainly identified, in two places, it is two and a half metres (over eight feet) thick. The C town was poorer than D; the individual houses so far excavated in C were, however, better built than the lower class houses of D. Grain-pits were interspersed among the houses, though not to the same extent as in the following period (B).

In the second campaign we noted that there were two successive phases of construction in the excavated portion of C; in the third campaign, in which we excavated a much larger area, we were able to follow these two phases over nearly the whole area, and to distinguish a new burned level which separated them in many places. While this burned layer is not so continuous as in other levels, there can be no doubt that C_1 was destroyed more or less completely in the fifteenth century B. C., a century or more after the destruction of D. This former destruction we were able to date roughly because of the following considerations. Just under the thick burned layer of C_2 (the second phase of C) we discovered a steatite scarab of Amenophis III (cir. 1411–1375 B. C.), with the inscription " Nib-mu'a-Rê', good god, lord of the two lands, who rises in every foreign land." [57] This scarab had belonged to a royal official of this king, and part of the copper ring on which it was set still adhered to it when found. This object proves conclusively, of course, that the layer of ashes over C_2 is later than about 1400 B. C.; it indicates that C_2 was occupied before 1375 B. C., and would prove it abso-

lutely if we were certain that it had not been reused.
Since it was found on its ring, and it bears an official
legend, the chances that it was reused are very small;
we merely mention the case to show what care must
be employed by the archæologist in the interpretation
of his material. Fortunately, however, all the potsherds found in C belong without question to the Late
Bronze Age, and correspond exactly to the pottery
discovered in the Tuthmosis III–Ramesses II strata
at Beth-shan. Moreover, the sherds found in C_1, so
far as they are different from those in C_2, belong in
the earliest part of the Late Bronze Age, as is clear
from a comparison of the Beth-shan material, as well
as from a study of other sites in Palestine. In C_2 appears the first Mycenæan pottery, imported into Egypt
and Palestine from the second half of the fifteenth
century to the latter part of the thirteenth. We are,
accordingly, justified in placing the fall of C_1 before
1400, but just when we cannot yet say. A scarab of
undoubted Ramesside date,[58] found in the débris of
C, helps us to date the close of this period after cir.
1250, while the complete absence of all characteristic
Cypro-Phœnician and Mycenæan ware in the B
stratum, which followed immediately upon the C level,
warns us that we must go down as far as possible
toward 1200 in fixing this date.

Our most remarkable discoveries in city C were
made just before the end of the third campaign: a
stone lion and a stone table of offerings, with three
lions in relief around the rim.[59] The lion is of *mizzī*
limestone, and is nearly sixty centimetres long; it is
represented couchant, with the two front paws parallel,
while the tail is curved gracefully over its back. It
is particularly interesting, despite the crudeness of its

execution, because of being the first stone lion of monumental size to be found in any early ruins of Palestine proper, the nearest one being the larger (and later?) lion of Karnaim (Sheikh Sa'd) in Bashan.[60] The table or bowl of offerings is of a softer limestone, and is a little less than thirty centimetres (one foot) in diameter. From the front of the rim there projects a very conventional lion's head, while the two front legs extend in both directions along the rim. The other two smaller lions are extended along the rim at the back of the bowl, so that both hind and front legs are stretched out at full length. In both cases the artistic execution is exceedingly crude, but entirely local; nothing resembling their execution has so far been found in any country of the Near East. Like the terra cotta altar-stands of Beth-shan, they belong to a local Canaanite art of a very provincial type. Ultimately, both the lion and the table of offerings undoubtedly descend from Egyptian prototypes, a relationship which is quite effectually concealed by the complete failure to observe Egyptian artistic conventions. Both of them were found standing on end in a vacant area, full of débris of the C period, and without any remains of foundation walls. It is obvious that they must have been thrown out from a temple, or building of a sacral nature, when C_2 was destroyed. The lion had been partly broken before it was thrown out. Thanks to their position with respect to the burned levels, and to the débris in which they were found, there can be no doubt whatever with regard to their date in C_2. Within the limits of the occupation of this city no clue to their exact age has been discovered, so we must be content with a date between 1500 and 1250 B. C.

While we have not yet discovered the Canaanite temple of this period, it lay presumably just outside of the area so far excavated, and may perhaps be found in our fourth campaign. The lion is obviously too small to have formed one of a pair of apotropæic guardians of the temple portal, so we may suppose that it was one of a pair which originally stood in some relation to the image of the deity worshipped in the temple. The lions may have flanked the pedestal or throne, or they may have stood in front of it; there are numerous analogies for both positions.[61]   In iconography the Syrian lion-god or lion-goddess generally stands on a lion, or sits on a throne supported by two lions, but the lions may also accompany the deity.[62]   One may speculate with regard to the nature of the divinity worshipped in the C city, and suggest that it was a lion-deity like Atargatis, or like the gods Makal and Ginai, revered at Beth-shan and at Heliopolis in Syria. 'Anat, consort of Makal at Beth-shan, was a serpent-goddess,[63] like the divinity of Tell Beit Mirsim in the D period, a fact which also points to a connection. Both Makal and Ginai were forms of Rashap (Resheph),[64] lord of the underworld, and 'Anat was primarily also a chthonic deity.[65] Beyond a suggestion one cannot, however, go at present.

In the C stratum we have so far discovered several different types of Astarte figurines, each illustrated by good examples, and some of unique iconographic value. We have so far found at least six Astarte plaques representing the naked Syrian goddess (dea genetrix) with spiral locks, without a head-dress, and holding a long stemmed lotus flower in each of her upraised hands. This type is found frequently in Astarte figurines from different parts of Palestine and

from the Late Bronze Age.[66] Our observations at
Tell Beit Mirsim warn us against dating it in the Iron
Age. The Canaanite appellation of this type of
goddess we know from a number of Egyptian monu-
ments of the New Empire, all from between 1400 and
1200,[67] representing her as standing on a lion, and
naming her *Qadesh,* that is, "courtesan" (Hebrew
qedeshah).[68] Qadesh was naturally the personifica-
tion of the *vis genetrix naturæ,* the native fertility of
the earth, which yields itself to every fecundizing
agency, as a woman with many husbands, yet perpet-
ually virgin.[69] We have above described the relief of
the serpent-goddess from stratum D, and pointed out a
number of very interesting parallels, which establish
the nature of the goddess and her symbolism beyond
all cavil.

Even more important from the comparative archæological point of view is the second type, which is
closely related to the first. This category is essentially
the same as the preceding, but substitutes a lofty
feather-crown for the uncovered head of Qadesh.
That it is of somewhat more recent origin is perhaps
indicated by the fact that the spiral locks have become
straight locks, ending at the breasts instead of curl-
ing around them. Like the preceding type it is evidently modelled after some popular idol, presumably
belonging to an important shrine. It has elsewhere
been suggested that the first type may reflect the
"Lady of Byblos" (Ba'alat Gubal of the Canaanites)[70]; the second one eludes us, though she may have
been at home in Syria. The fact that the feathers are
perfectly distinct and cannot possibly be misinter-
preted enables us to explain other head-dresses of
Astarte figurines from Palestine and Mesopotamia,

which have hitherto been regarded erroneously as some sort of mural crown or calathus, as feather-crowns.[71] The writer has studied all the relevant material from Mesopotamia and the lands of the eastern Mediterranean basin, without reaching a definitive conclusion concerning the original home of this feather-crown. The latter makes its first appearance in Mesopotamia, north and south, as a symbol of deity shortly before the middle of the second millennium B. C., and enjoys a very extensive diffusion among the Babylonians (Cossæans), Assyrians, and Mitannians (Tell Ḥalâf, Biblican Gozan).[72] Ishtar is often represented with the feather-crown; sometimes also she wears the spiral ringlets. So far as we know, the feather head-dress had not been employed in Mesopotamia for any purposes since early Sumerian times.[73] On the other hand we find the feather-crown widely diffused in Asia Minor and Crete in a somewhat later period (Late Bronze and Early Iron). Certain of these types from Cyprus and Crete point to an eastern origin, while the Early Iron figurines of Artemis from Sparta are unquestionably derived from Cyprus and Phœnicia.[74] However, the feather-crowns of the Philistines and their congeners suggest an early profane use in Ægean and Anatolian lands,[75] and make it not unlikely that our feather-crown is of Anatolian origin. From Asia Minor it may have spread to Syria, from which it was diffused to the south and east in the first half of the second millennium, possibly during the Hyksos period.[76]

The remaining types of the C period are represented by one or two examples each, only one of which is complete enough to warrant elaborate comparisons. This one represents the *dea nuda* with her arms hang-

ing by her sides. Her hair is gathered into two heavy
masses which hang down on the shoulders. Around
the navel is a circle of about ten round marks, which
may portray tattoo marks in imitation of an actual
custom among women. A very similar figurine, found
in a late Middle Bronze context in Egypt, but of
Asiatic origin, exhibits precisely the same circle of
dots around the navel.[77]

It must be emphasized that these figurines are all of
religious or magical character, and are none of them
toys. Toys did not come into general use until the
Iron Age, the period of Israelite occupation. In
Mesopotamia toys are also unknown until a comparatively late date.[78] Even in Egypt a large proportion
of the objects which are commonly considered to be
playthings for children are really amulets. It should
also be stressed that the Astarte figurines of the
Bronze Age, though used as amulets to protect women
in child-birth and to give fecundity to sterile wives,
etc., were actually representations of known images of
the Syrian goddess. In some cases it is, of course,
quite possible that the prototype was unknown to the
people who employed their icons as amulets. It is not
until the early Israelite period that we find figurines
which cannot well be regarded as representations of
specific idol types, but which seem to be abstract per-
sonifications or impersonal symbols. These cases we
shall describe below.

To what stock the inhabitants of Tell Beit Mirsim
in the Late Bronze Age belonged eludes our knowledge. That they were a typically " Canaanite " group
seems to be clear, since they did not differ in any
tangible respect from the contemporaneous occupants
of other towns in Palestine. For the near-by towns of

Keilah, Lachish, and Tell el-Ḥesī, we have documentary material in the Amarna Tablets and a locally found cuneiform letter.[79]   According to these sources, the population of the Shephelah was just as mixed as that of other parts of the country: Amorite names are found with Indo-Iranian, Hurrian with Canaanite.[80] The language of the people was Canaanite (Hebrew). The Egyptian and cuneiform evidence is so definite, and the results of archæological explanation so thoroughly in accord with it, that we cannot possibly regard stratum C as dating from after the conquest of the Shephelah described in Joshua—unless we reject the early historical traditions of Israel almost completely.[81]

Less, however, can be said about the social organization of the period.   So far no houses of nobles have been found in level C; on the other hand, the houses of the lower class are much better than in stratum D, which represents the feudal age *par excellence*.   It is evident, to judge from the discoveries made in different parts of Palestine,[82] that there was a gradual decline of the nobility, accompanied by a rise of certain elements of the lower class, during the Late Bronze Age.   This change may be referred with entire confidence to the Egyptian rule in Palestine, which bore with increasing weight on the nobility, especially after the fifteenth century.   Taxes, often ruinous, were borne by the nobles—since there was no other class of importance.   The nobility had to pay the royal taxes, plus the bribes required to satisfy a chronically rapacious hierarchy of Egyptian officials,[83] and in addition to the heavy burden of the mercenary garrisons and their commanders.[84]   Furthermore, they were constantly subject to the duties of furnishing supplies to the royal armies marching into Asia along the edge of the Shephelah[85] and of providing serfs for the corvée.[86]   At the same time that the noble class declined, the strength of the craftsmen grew, relatively speaking, because of the increasing development of commerce.   Commercial relations between Egypt and Asia grew steadily, and at the same time we find a marked tendency to industrial specialization in certain Canaanite towns,[87] a tendency which brought increase in trade with it.   It is, however, quite impossible, with our present knowledge, to determine what the status of craftsmen was, whether they were liberated slaves or semi-free serfs.   It is possible that they even achieved a certain degree of absolute freedom, in so far as this would be compatible with life in a town under a feudal constitution.   Public security was, however, less than in D, doubtless because of the decreased prestige of the local princes, together with the indifference of the Egyptian authorities.   The increasing strength of the semi-nomadic Khabiru, who occupied most of the hill-country, undoubtedly contributed largely to the lack of security, so vividly illustrated by the Amarna letters from Palestine.[88]

As already shown, the fall of the C town must be dated in the second half of the thirteenth century— exactly when we cannot as yet say.   It may eventually be possible to fix its date more precisely, when we can date the conquest of the Shephelah by Israel.   At present our only absolute datum is still the reference to the defeat of the people of Israel by Menephthes (before his fifth year, which fell somewhere between 1230 and 1220 B. C.).   In spite of all that has lately been written in favour of a higher date for the principal phase of the Conquest, it is very difficult to

reconcile the traditions of Israel with a date before
the latter part of the reign of Ramesses the Great,
i. e., before 1250 B. C. at the earliest. Whether the
Canaanite town of Tell Beit Mirsim was destroyed
before or after the "defeat" of Israel by the Egyptians is naturally impossible to determine with our
present knowledge. Archæologically, however, it is
certain that a major break in the continuity of culture
lies between C and B. This break is not due to an
interruption in the occupation of the place; on the
contrary, the new city walls and the house foundations
were laid in the ashes of the preceding conflagration,
a fact confirmed again and again as our excavation of
the site progresses. No appreciable interval can thus
have intervened between destruction and reoccupation,
quite the opposite of what we find between D and C.

8.   THE EARLY ISRAELITE OCCUPATION (B)

The most remarkable change in the character of B
when compared to C is the complete alteration in the
construction of the city wall. Instead of the relatively
massive Bronze Age walls, which vary at our site
from eight to fifteen feet in thickness (2.5 to 4.5 m.),
we find that the main city wall of the Iron Age is
only five feet thick. Since this width was evidently
too little for safety, a system of casemates was introduced, consisting of an uninterrupted line of closed
or open chambers between the outer wall and a thin
inner wall, no more than 2½ feet thick (like an
ordinary house wall). Thin transverse walls separated the casemate rooms from one another. Some of
them were closed, and nothing but earth and stones
was found in them, while most had been employed
as magazines belonging to the adjacent houses, the

upper part of which may have overlooked the city wall. The sloping external revetment of the city wall was repaired with much smaller stones than had been used in the Canaanite age. This wall was undoubtedly built immediately after the destruction of C, since its foundations were laid in the ashes of the conflagration which destroyed the former, as we have already observed. The foundations and substructure continued in use until the final destruction of the city by the Chaldæans, more than six centuries later. It is very interesting to note that the width of five feet (sometimes six to seven feet) is absolutely characteristic of Israelite city walls, the exceptions being due either to the importance of the place fortified, as at Jerusalem, or to the continued use of Bronze Age fortifications, as at Tell en-Naṣbeh (southern side). This change in the strength of walls is not due to any parallel development in surrounding lands, nor to the increase of public security (in the time of the Judges!), but evidently to a complete alteration in social organization. Under the loose patriarchal form of Israelite society there was no systematic coercion of the individual; "every man did what was right in his own eyes." The corvée was unknown.[89] It was, therefore, as a rule manifestly impossible to induce the inhabitants of an early Israelite town to submit to the prolonged and difficult labour of constructing a massive city wall. The Israelite wall of Jerusalem was not built until the tenth century, when captives were available for the corvée. Solomon introduced the corvée into Israel, but even he was apparently very circumspect in his use of free-born Israelites for forced labour.[90]

Our most remarkable discovery in stratum B was a

very large number of grain-pits or silos (in the original sense of the term), which we struck wherever our excavations reached the B level. The largest found were about ten feet (three metres) in diameter on the inside. Their construction was simple: pits were dug, lined with a circular stone wall, like a well-shaft, and generally floored with stones, while the interior surface was entirely coated with ḥawârah,[91] the same material as that used for the outside of roofs down to the present day. Each twenty-metre square of our excavation generally contained several of these grain-pits. At first they distressed us greatly, in view of the damage to the lower strata which they cause. Happily, however, the bottom of the pit was often found to be above stratum D, our most important level, a fact which has cheered us greatly. Moreover, our silos have proved to yield invaluable evidence for the demarcation of distinct phases within period B. They were constructed at different times, some intersecting older silos from the same period, and were abandoned at different times, especially when the wall collapsed, as frequently happened. The débris with which the unbroken part of the silo was filled, within a very short time after its abandonment, contains broken pottery belonging almost exclusively to the B period, and naturally older than the time of abandonment. From a careful comparative study of different silos—numbering several score—we have been able to distinguish clearly between three phases of B. The results of our second campaign have been in this respect fully confirmed by the material discovered in our third. Besides, we have now been able to parallel the evidence from grain-pits by evidence from houses and from successive phases of construction.

There were three clear phases in B, respectively pre-Philistine (B_1), Philistine (B_2), and post-Philistine (B_3). The first is characterized by the complete absence of Philistine pottery and of vases influenced by it.[92] We have no tilted horizontal loop handles, no Philistine decoration. The Philistine beer jugs with swan friezes and wine craters with friezes of checkers, Maltese crosses, and spirals are both entirely missing. On the other hand this phase is equally devoid of Mycenæan sherds, of base-ring biscuit ware, of wishbone-handled bowls with seam patterns, etc., which are ubiquitous in C. It is true that we have a few late local imitations, which hardly resemble the originals at all. The ware of phase B_1 is almost exclusively composed of transitional local forms, still distinctly Late Bronze, but indicating a complete loss of the artistic tradition in decoration, such as it was, and an absolute cessation of imports of pottery from the coast. It is true that the Bronze Age types just referred to did not continue long in Canaanite (Phœnician) districts, but soon gave way (in the twelfth century) to Iron Age types, running parallel with Philistine ceramics, but there was apparently no such intervening phase as that to which we have just called attention. A similar interruption of imported pottery was observed at Beth-shemesh by Mackenzie. On the coast, at Ashkelon and Gerar, Phythian-Adams and Petrie have observed an abrupt shift, but no trace (hitherto) of our intervening phase; Cypro-Phœnician ware is replaced suddenly by Philistine, with no indication of a period in which the former gradually yielded to the latter.[93] We are consequently forced to conclude that B_1 represents the first period of the Israelite occupation, before the broken lines of communication had been reëstablished, and before new commercial relations had been formed. The duration of the period is uncertain; the lowest reasonable estimate is a generation, the highest two or three generations, if we judge by such ambiguous indications as the relative amount of pottery from this phase which we have found. As has already been shown, the period probably began before 1200; its end must fall soon after the Philistine occupation of the coastal plain, an event which took place between 1190 and 1160.[94] If we date the extension of Philistine power into the Shephelah about 1150 B. C., we cannot be more than a decade or two from the truth.

The second phase (B_2) is characterized by an abundance of imported Philistine pottery and of local wares influenced by it or by new types of Iron Age pottery from the north. The pottery becomes unmistakably Iron Age in its general appearance; pebble-burnishing, which had almost died out during the Late Bronze Age, comes back into vogue, but is done by hand, without the use of the potter's wheel. This phase clearly represents the period of Philistine domination, during most of which the Shephelah was subject to the tyranny of the Ægean pentapolis. It is followed, after a period of considerable length, judging from such general considerations as those which we employed in order to get an idea of the duration of B_1, by the third phase of B, in which Philistine pottery in the narrow sense vanishes, and we reach the transition from Early Iron I to Early Iron II. B_3 belongs in the tenth century; historically we can fix the end of Philistine influence during the reign of Saul (cir. 1020–1000) and David (cir. 1000–960 B. C.), so we may date the transition from B_2 to

B_3 roughly about 1000 B. C. During B_3 pebble-burnishing improves greatly in technique, and the wheel is employed for the burnishing operation as well as for the moulding of the vessel itself. By holding the burnishing tool firmly, and moving it slowly down the inside of a bowl, the potter produced a continuous spiral, which gives the superficial effect of concentric rings, whence the term " ring-burnishing." Ring-burnishing began in the tenth century, and replaced hand burnishing of bowls almost entirely in the ninth century.[95] There is a coarseness about the lines of this early ring-burnishing, when compared to later work (from about 800 on), which furnishes a very convenient *point d'appui.* The comparison of the latest pottery of B_3 with the earliest of the A period, which followed it without an appreciable lacuna in the occupation, shows clearly that we cannot place the destruction of B before the latter part of the tenth century, nor after the beginning of the ninth. Since there is only one historical invasion with which to reckon between the middle of David's reign (cir. 980) and the invasion of Sennacherib, namely the conquest of Judah by Shishak, in the fifth year of Rehoboam (cir. 920 B. C.),[96] we are on safe ground in combining the two events. Shishak captured the fortified towns of Judah, including Jerusalem, as we are assured both by the Bible and by his own inscriptions, to which we must add one found by Fisher at Megiddo.[97] Since his army was composed of barbarian mercenaries, and Tell Beit Mirsim was situated in the part of Judah which was exposed to the first fury of the onslaught, the completeness of the destruction becomes readily intelligible. Some details will be given below.

An interesting illustration of our chronology is furnished by a broken bit of pottery which originally contained a name, perhaps of its original owner, incised neatly on it. Two characters are left, one entirely preserved; it is a beautiful archaic *kaf,* the first one found on Palestinian soil, though several inscriptions containing it have been discovered since the War in Phœnicia. This particular form of *kaf* never appears in inscriptions from the ninth century or later, and disappeared in southern Palestine even before the time of the Gezer Calendar, which itself antedates the ninth century, as we know from the archaic *mem* which it contains.[98] Unfortunately, we cannot be sure, owing to the circumstances of discovery, just where in the history of B our sherd belongs—probably to B_3, *i. e.,* to the tenth century B. C. While this sherd does not enable us to date with greater accuracy than would be possible on the basis of the pottery alone, it offers the historian who is not an archæologist a welcome confirmation of our ceramic chronology.

The grain-pits to which we have referred seem to be found almost exclusively in C and B; none have been found so far in D or earlier periods. After the earliest phase of A they again vanish; even in the beginning of A the few which we have found are much smaller than in B, and were obviously not intended as regular granaries. In B we have at least twice as many grain-pits as in C, and, as already shown, they belong to all its phases. There can be no doubt that the abundance of grain-pits, as well as their size, illustrates the insecurity of property in Israel in the time of the Judges. With no organized system of defense, the people of a border town like our site were exposed to constant raids, both by nomadic Midianites or Amalekites and by Philistines,[99] so it was necessary to protect the grain by concealing it in safe places within the walls of the town.

Some very interesting and important discoveries bearing on the religious life of Israel during this period have been made. A small limestone altar of incense, of which only the top (measuring 7 by 9 cm. in horizontal section) is preserved, has four projections, called "horns" by the Hebrews, at its four corners. Examples of similar, but larger and more elaborate limestone altars of incense have been found elsewhere in Palestine in recent years, especially at Shechem and Megiddo.[100] Since our specimen cannot be later than the tenth century, these others, belonging to the seventh century for the most part, are at least 250 years younger.[101] Löhr, Wiener, and others have maintained that these discoveries prove that the Wellhausen position with regard to the use of incense in the official ritual of Israel is entirely wrong.[102] According to Wellhausen, incense was not employed in the Mosaic ritual until the Babylonian Exile, when it appears in the Priest-code.[103] Unfortunately for this otherwise rather impressive argument against Wellhausen, Ingholt recently discovered an altar of incense in Palmyra, bearing an inscription which proves that the name of this object was *hammân*.[104] Now the same word occurs frequently in the Bible as the name of an objectionable pagan cult-object, against the use of which Isaiah and later writers inveighed. Hitherto the word *hammân* has been rendered most enigmatically "sun-pillar"—a translation which was quite meaningless to the archæologist. We therefore note that the altars of incense found in Palestine, so far from disproving Wellhausen's view on this particular point, help materially to prove its correctness.

On the other hand, they explain why incense was not used in the ritual employed by the official Mosaic religion of Israel; it was too closely bound up with objectionable pagan practices. At the same time, accordingly, this group of archæological discoveries supports the results of the documentary hypothesis and eliminates one of the principal arguments against the originality and uniqueness of Mosaism! [105]

A respectable number of Astarte figurines was discovered in B, but not so many as in either C or A. Aside from a few nondescript figurines of the *dea nuda*, not always of certain provenance, though quite distinct from the types of the Canaanite age, the most important were a group of five figurines, all made in different moulds, and all representing a naked woman in the process of accouchement. One was complete, one other was nearly so, while the remaining three were only torsos or fragments. This type has apparently never been found before; at least no examples have been published, and no archæologist who has seen them was acquainted with parallels. Examination by gynæcologists has yielded a number of varying explanations in matters of detail. The figure has a distended abdomen, but small breasts. Her hands are clasped firmly, almost convulsively, below her abdomen. The navel projects abnormally for a primipara, and suggests that the figure may represent a woman who has borne children. There is an exaggerated protrusion of the vulvar region, which cannot denote a pathological condition, but must be an attempt to suggest the descent of the child's head and the imminence of delivery. The smallness of the breasts is evidently intended to accentuate the distention of the womb. It is most unlikely that our figure represents the *dea*

Syria in any of her aspects, since there is an entire absence of any cult symbolism. It rather portrays a normal woman, with braided locks hanging down on the shoulders and three bracelets on each wrist. It accordingly seems most likely that these figures were merely intended to hasten parturition by sympathetic magic, and that their generic resemblance to Canaanite Astarte figurines is due to the fact that they were used for a similar purpose. It is reasonable to suppose that they also served as charms to bring fruitfulness to barren women.

In a silo of the Philistine period, and consequently belonging probably to the eleventh century B. C., we found the torso of a hollow figurine, representing a nude female with prominent breasts, pressing a dove with outstretched wings to her bosom. This figure obviously formed part of a small vase, like later Greek figurines representing Aphrodite, clad in archaic costume and holding a dove in one arm, which were used as perfume containers.[106] They are found in Cyprus, Rhodes, and other Greek lands, and are dated between the seventh and the fifth centuries B. C.[107] Our example illustrates an early form of the same type of perfume vase, some three centuries before its appearance in Greek lands under Cypro-Phœnician influence. Bronze Age figurines of the *dea nuda* which have been found in Cyprus, and which portray a goddess with enormous ear-flaps and earrings, sometimes show her pressing a dove with outstretched wings to her bosom, between her breasts, in exactly the same way.[108] Other figurines of this latter type, but without the dove, have been found in Palestine, showing that, like most characteristic objects of Cypro-Phœnician origin, they were diffused over the entire region occupied or directly influenced by Canaanite culture.[109] That none of these figurines discovered in Palestine so far exhibit the dove can only be regarded as a coincidence. As is well known, the dove was sacred to Astarte in Syria and Palestine as well as in Cyprus, where the cult of Paphian Aphrodite, the goddess of the dove, was exceedingly popular in the Iron Age.[110] In our figurines the function of the dove is evidently similar to that of the serpent in Bronze Age idols, as already described above.[111] While it is very possible that the cult of the dove-goddess entered Israel under Philistine influence,[112] and the local origin of the figurine is suggested by its clay, it is also quite possible that our object was imported from outside as a vessel of perfume. At all events, it is not only archæologically important, but is also significant as illustrating the forms of religious and iconographical influence then exercised by the Canaanites and Philistines on the Israelites.

Not much of exceptional interest to the student of the Bible was discovered in our B stratum outside of the objects which we have already discussed. The first iron tools and weapons appeared in this level. Iron sickles and ploughshares, or rather plough-tips, illustrate the commencement of the Iron Age.[113] The relatively high cost of iron is perhaps shown by the small size of these instruments, when compared to similar ones of the A level; it is, however, possible that the small size is simply due to imitation of bronze or copper models. As is well known, the Philistines maintained a monopoly of the importation and forging of iron, and their " corner " was not broken until the reign of Saul (cir. 1020 B. c.).[114] We cannot tell whether our iron from Tell Beit Mirsim antedates the time of Saul or not; probably it comes from the tenth century, when Israelites enjoyed the free use of this important metal.[115]

Some curious illustrations of the "art" of the period were found in tenth century context. One was the painted outline of a dragon, on a large potsherd; it was unfortunately not complete, the hind-quarters and tail being broken off. The dragon has an elongated body, the legs and feet of a fowl, and a bird's head. The head is turned so that the animal looks back over its shoulder, two plumes falling over its bill, while a peculiar crest in the shape of a duck-bill protrudes from the back of the head (facing forward). It has analogies both with the Babylonian *mushkhusshû,* a crested serpent with four legs (the front legs being leonine and the hind legs aquiline),[116] and with the Egyptian *sefer,* a quadruped with a bird's head, two wings, and a long tail.[117] The crest suggests the former; the bird's head resembles the latter. It has been suggested that the Babylonian *mushkhusshû* may be the prototype of the Israelite symbolical seraph, but the latter had wings.[118] Another illustration of Israelite or Canaanite art of this age is a seal-stone of scaraboid shape in red marble, showing a man between two ostriches, which he grasps by the neck. This motive became popular in Assyrian cylinders some centuries later, where a winged god is shown in the same way.[119] We have here the oldest datable example of this type, which evidently has some mythical background, as yet not recovered.

The destruction of the B city by the barbarian mercenaries of Shishak was accompanied by a more or less thorough demolition of the fortifications, which we can see vividly at the two gates. The West Gate was almost completely razed, and it is even uncertain whether the A builders followed the same plan of construction or not. At the East Gate the super-structure was destroyed, and the new builders employed a new plan in part. Where the old house foundations were still preserved, they were reused, but in most cases entirely new foundations had to be laid. After the third campaign it has become certain that the site was not abandoned, but that the old settlers returned to their homes soon after the withdrawal of the Egyptians. The new foundations were often laid in the ashes of the conflagration, just as in the case of city B. The fact that no bodies were found in the ruins of B may indicate that the inhabitants of the city fled into the almost impenetrable mountain gorges to the northwest of the city, and that the invaders found it empty. However this may be, there cannot be the slightest doubt about the completeness of the destruction or about the short duration of the abandonment, as shown above.

9. THE PERIOD OF THE JEWISH MONARCHY

The long history of city A, which lasted for more than three centuries (maximum duration about 330 years) warns us against trying to generalize. Since its growth and final decline are part of that history, most of our description must be taken as applying to the town of the late eighth and the early seventh century, before the final decline set in. Happily for the accuracy of our description, we find so many objects of the same kind, and so few corresponding objects of a different type, that there can be no doubt with regard to the chief material elements of culture during the age of maximum prosperity.

During so long a period of uninterrupted occupation we must expect much rebuilding and restoration. In some places we find that there are three phases of construction, each characterized by different plans, or making important alterations in the old plans. In some cases we find that buildings were entirely abandoned, and not replaced at all. More frequently we find that inferior structures have been replaced by better ones, or that partly empty or entirely vacant spaces have been occupied by houses. At the very end of the history of the town we find increasing carelessness in building; wretched walls are raised, and once we have a somewhat massive, but very poor building replacing well-built houses. A curious fact is that the inside floors of houses did not rise appreciably in level, for the most part, during the long history of the town, while the street level outside nearly always shows a considerable rise in level, often reaching three feet or more (a metre). The street level did not rise gradually because of lack of cleaning; it rose in irregular phases, evidently after the collapse of houses, either because of earthquake or of poor construction. In general, any house construction might be expected to result in the rise of the street level, because of the inevitable accumulation of material and débris in the adjacent street.

The most interesting innovation of the latest city was an entirely new type of house construction, also found in other sites of southern Palestine, but not hitherto recognized.[120] This new type can hardly be derived directly from either the " hearth-house " (megaron) of the north or from the " court-house " of the south.[121] The former is illustrated by excellent examples from Beth-shemesh and Ataroth (Tell

en-Naṣbeh); our house-plans from level B are too
defective to yield much information. The latter is
well illustrated by the houses from G and D which
we have described above. The new type of A is
characterized by the presence of a large room, seldom
smaller than 30 square metres (330 square feet), at
the sides of which are from two to four small rooms,
serving evidently as storage chambers. Along the
long axis of the room are set three or four—usually
four—stone pillars for the support of the ceiling.
These pillars were generally hewn in a roughly rectangular, sometimes oval section, and varied from
1.50 to 1.80 metres in height (*i. e.,* five to six feet).
Since the height of the room was about two metres
or a little more (six and a half to seven feet), the
pillar stones were often set on an equally rude stylo-
bate. Occasionally we find a more elegant execution,
resembling that of the pillars in the stables of Solomon at Megiddo, which are at present the oldest, as
well as the best examples of this type of construction.[122] In view of its introduction at the time of
Solomon, we may perhaps ascribe it to the Phœnicians,
to whom so many innovations of the Iron Age in
Palestine were due.[123] So far we have cleared scores
of these pillar alignments; practically every house
possessed one, though some exhibit large stones piled
on one another like pillar drums instead of monoliths.
It gives one a new respect for the native energy and
industry of these Judæan peasants when one considers
that each house, as a rule, had four such monoliths,
weighing from 800 to 1400 kilos (from 1800 to 3100
pounds) each. Each stone had to be hewn at the
quarry, dragged to the foot of the hill and up the
hill into the town, and set up in place. And yet the

inhabitants were simple peasants! It is quite impossible to imagine the modern Arab peasantry of Palestine as willing to undertake such an arduous method of construction in their own houses.

The inmates of the house lived in the second story, to which access was generally obtained by a well-built outside stone staircase. In some cases we are entirely justified in assuming that there was a third story (perhaps only a half-story), since the solidity of the pillars in the ground floor would otherwise remain an enigma. The walls of the upper part of the house were built of adobe brick or of wood, instead of stone, which was used in the lower part of the walls. Occasionally we find partition walls of adobe even in the first floor. The ceilings and roof were all of wood; the vaulting of the modern Near East was wholly unknown. The intensity of the conflagration which destroyed the A level is easily explained when we realize how much wood was employed in construction. Modern Arab houses cannot be damaged by fire; Palestinian Arab boys find the greatest difficulty in understanding how ancient cities were destroyed by conflagration. The walls were plastered with lime, and the floor was often paved with small stones, though the inmates lived and slept upstairs, so paving was unnecessary.

The houses were closely crowded together, with only the smallest courts—if we can give this name to narrow passages and tiny open areas at the entrance-gate from the street. Streets were mostly narrow—seldom more than seven feet wide—and were only occasionally paved with small stones. We may estimate the entire population of the town at between 2500 and 5000, by allowing ten persons—four adults and six children—to each large house, occupying about 150 square metres (including the adjacent street areas), while smaller houses would naturally have a correspondingly smaller number of occupants. The area of the town within the walls was not quite 3.5 hectares (about eight acres), which contained between 250 and 350 houses. However, as at Tell en-Naṣbeh, the population overflowed the walled area, and we find house remains on the threshing-floors to the south, and elsewhere in the vicinity of the city. While, as we shall see presently, sanitary conditions must have been good, when compared to those in a modern Arab village, disease would have become rife unless the inhabitants of the ancient town resembled the present Ruba'îyeh. The latter, as we have seen above, nearly all own houses in Dûrā, but during almost the entire year they live in caves, tents, and booths (Hebrew *sukkôth*) near their land, returning in midsummer to Dûrā, and leaving again after the winter rains set in. While the territory of the ancient town was much smaller, it must have extended for five miles from north to south, and for eight to ten miles from east to west. It is, therefore, entirely safe to suppose, both from Biblical parallels, from the exigencies of the case, and from modern conditions in the same district, that most of the inhabitants spent part, if not most of the year outside their city.

We have spoken of the sanitary conditions in antiquity. It is true that there was, of course, no modern system of sewage. Otherwise matters were much better than they would be to-day. No cattle were kept in the city; sheep, goats, and large cattle remained outside of the walls in their folds and enclosures. Nowhere have we found the remains of

sheepfolds or ancient manure heaps in the area of
A. There were many cisterns inside the walls, in
order to supplement the water supply of the wells
outside the city. These cisterns were, however, nearly
always provided with cement settling basins, and a
number of well-constructed water channels were
traced. The cistern water appears to have come from
the house-roofs, though we cannot say positively that
this was its only source. A great many stone roof-
rollers have been found in our excavation; they are
characteristically more massive than those employed
by the Arabs to-day. While the streets were not
regularly drained, we have found a drainage channel
running from the interior of the town through the
East Gate to the outside of the city.[124]

The city was entered by two gates, one in the east,
the other opposite it, in the western side. The East
Gate, which stood on the site of the old Bronze Age
gateway, exhibits the same indirect ingress which we
find in Islamic city gates; it makes two bends at right
angles, in order to avert the possibility that a direct
arrow fire from outside might command the main
gate. The width of the gateway is only two metres
(less than seven feet) at its narrowest point, so that
it would barely admit a chariot drawn by two horses.
The West Gate is even narrower, being only a metre
wide, so that only pedestrians and laden asses might
enter by it. Yet the West Gate was apparently the
meeting place of the local magistrates, who transacted
business in a commodious and well-built tower just
north of the gate. The tower measures slightly over
13 x 12 metres (43 by 40 feet) on the inside. It
was entered by a broad doorway from the interior of
the town, which led into a court, around which were

six rooms. In the tower we found several standard weights, particularly a beautiful eight mina weight of polished limestone, perfectly preserved, and hence of metrological value.[125] It is clear that standard weights were among the most necessary articles in a hall of justice.

Like other towns of Judah in the late pre-exilic period, ours was devoted to a special industry, in addition to its ordinary peasant occupations. In this case it was the woollen textile industry—the spinning, weaving, and dyeing of woollen stuffs. In part it was doubtless the proximity to the Negeb, the dry land of the south, over which pastured great herds of sheep, that led to the choice of this particular industry. It must not be supposed that the people of the town were divided into two classes, farmers and craftsmen; on the contrary, everything points to a double occupation, farming and the manufacture of woollen goods. Vast quantities of clay loom-weights have been dug up in our three campaigns, showing that there must have been a loom in nearly every house. We have so far discovered six dye-plants, four of which follow a definite plan of construction and arrangement, which may, therefore, be considered as standard. These dye-plants are the first to have been found in Palestine; the native labourers recognized them before we did, and gave them the correct name *maṣbaghah*. In rectangular rooms, all of which, wherever located, have approximately the same dimensions, three metres by six (ten by twenty feet), one end is occupied by two massive dye-vats, with shallow basins of cement adjoining them. In the two corners nearest the vats we invariably found hole-mouth jars containing lime. The dye-vats are made of single stones about three

feet high (80 cm. to a metre) and the same in
diameter, hewn round, but with flat tops and bottoms.
The interior is hollowed out to form a roughly
spherical basin, about a foot and a half (40–50 cm.)
across, with a narrow mouth, seldom over six inches
across (20–25 cm.). Around the rim there runs a
deep circular channel with a hole in its bottom communicating with the interior of the vat; we generally
found a stone fitted into the hole. The purpose of
the channel was naturally to catch the precious dye
when it was spilled on the rim, and to return it to
the vat. Near the vats, in the part of the room otherwise unoccupied by the installation, we generally
found a number of large stones, about fifteen or
sixteen inches across, all pierced with a hole through
the center.

A careful study of the dye-plants of Hebron has
led to some interesting results. To-day much is naturally different. The introduction of indigo from
the East has greatly reduced the cost of dye, and has
practically driven out the use of other dyes for woollen
garments. The simplest mode of dyeing still requires
the use of two vats, just as in antiquity, but there are
a number of more prolonged manipulations which require several additional vats, employed when better—
and more costly—products are demanded. But the
modern vat is a flimsy structure, formed by a large
earthenware pot set in a bench of brick, stone, and
plaster. It is interesting to note that our very first
dye-plant found at Tell Beit Mirsim was made in
the same way. The standard vat was hewn to last for
ever—another striking illustration of the great energy
displayed by the pre-exilic Judæans when compared
with the modern inhabitants of southern Palestine.

Lime is still employed for the purpose of fixing the dye, just as in antiquity. We have so far been unable to find any satisfactory explanation of the perforated stones, which have no modern analogy. Since they invariably lie in a single line, we first supposed that they formed an aqueduct for water used in treating the cloth. No such aqueduct has been found, however, and the sides of the stones do not fit together, nor has any lime plaster been found on them, so it would appear that they were employed as pressure weights, perhaps to press the dye out of the cloth, in order to conserve it.[126]

Turning from the industry of the town to other features of the life of its people, we shall describe the Astarte figurines of the A period. More than a score have so far been found in stratum A, all of the same type, which held exclusive sway. This type is often called the pillar goddess, and represents a woman's head, bust, and arms, the lower part of the figurine being a simple column, spreading at the base, so that it might stand erect. The breasts are always very large and prominent, and the woman places her hands under them, as if presenting them to a nursing infant. This type of Astarte figurine unquestionably does portray a goddess, Ashtaroth as the *dea nutrix,* the protector of nursing mothers. Similar figurines are common in Phœnicia and Cyprus after the tenth century; from the north they spread southward into Palestine, evidently in the ninth century, after the Division of the Monarchy.[127] It is probable, however, that they were not regarded by the Israelites as icons of the Syrian goddess, but merely as potent amulets, like the figures of the B period which represent a woman in labour. They are interesting because of the remarkably fine execution of one or two specimens from our site, which are fully equal artistically to the best archaic Greek work.[128]   Incidentally, it may be added that the coiffure is not a conventional imitation of older work, but clearly portrays the style of the day. We can thus see that the Israelite women of the day plaited and curled their locks most elaborately, allowing the braided mass to hang down around the head below the ears. There is not the slightest basis for the statement sometimes made that these figurines have bobbed hair.

We have so far found about a dozen cosmetic palettes, all in stratum A. These palettes are circular, with a small flat base, a rounded cavity in the middle of the top, surrounded by a broad flat rim.[129] The rim is generally decorated with an intricate geometric design in incised work (originally coloured dark blue, at least in some cases), or is inlaid with little disks of dark blue gum. The effect of the blue decoration against the polished white limestone surface must have been quite striking. One palette was not decorated at all, but exhibited twelve rounded holes (with a hemispherical cross section) on the rim, in two of which there was still some powdered copper ore (malachite). These palettes were unquestionably employed in order to prepare the mineral substances contained in face-paints by powdering them with a bone, metal, or hæmatite spatula (we discovered one of the last named type in an earlier level); they are found in other Iron Age sites in Palestine, but never in such abundance as at our site. From Egyptian and other sources we can give details with regard to the use of different mineral substances on the face. Powdered *kuḥl* (*kohl*)[130] was used in order to paint the eye-

brows and eyelashes black; it was then made of manganese or antimony, whereas it is now mostly soot.[131]
The use of *kuhl* undoubtedly had a certain prophy-
lactic value in keeping infections out of the eye.
Powdered malachite or turquoise was employed to
paint the lower eyelids green.[132]   Finally, we may
safely suppose that powdered hæmatite clay (red
ochre) was used, as in Egypt, to enhance the natural
colour of the lips.[133]   Truly Isaiah was not without
justification when he denounced the frivolity of the
daughters of Zion (Isa. 3: 18–23).   It offers at least
some satisfaction to know that the ladies of to-day
content themselves generally with comparatively harm-
less paints and powders of organic origin!

Few inscriptions have been found in stratum A,
because all writing was ordinarily restricted to papyrus
and leather (parchment), substances which were naturally oxidized thousands of years ago in this damp
soil.   So far, despite the most assiduous search, we
have not discovered any true ostraca, *i. e.,* potsherds
inscribed in ink, or scratched with a sharp pointed
instrument.   We have, however, thanks to this careful
search,[134] found five fragments of vases which had
been inscribed with a short inscription, incised in the
wall of the vessel before it was broken.   Not one of
the inscriptions was complete, though in two cases
prolonged search brought to light three sherds belonging to each of two inscriptions.   All of them but one
are names of persons, evidently of the owner of the
vessel: Uzziah, Hezekiah, Nahum (or Menahem),
Gera (probably), all good Biblical names employed
in the period of the Divided Monarchy.[135]   The fifth
inscription from A contains the Hebrew word *bath,*
an eight gallon liquid measure; presumably the entire

inscription read " a *bath* of wine," or the like. All are written in the now familiar script of the Siloam inscription, and belong to the eighth or seventh century B. C. It is extremely interesting to learn that writing was used so commonly, even in every day life, by the Judæans of the late pre-exilic age.

Interesting light on the fiscal and administrative system of Judah in the same period is shed by the handles of large amphoras, stamped with an official seal, bearing the inscription "Belonging to the king— Hebron," four of which we discovered here. So far nearly two hundred stamped jar-handles of this type have been found in Judah, with four different place-names: Hebron, Socoh, Ziph, and Mamshath (a place in the Negeb, not mentioned in the Bible).[136] These four places were the administrative centers of four fiscal districts, probably established by Hezekiah.[137] The wine and oil delivered in payment of taxes ("tithes") were put into standard jars, probably holding a *bath,* and these standard jars, all stamped with the official seal, were then circulated as measures of value. Since nothing of the kind has been found outside the narrow limits of Judah, it appears that the idea was original there—another illustration of the originality of that little country in the days of the great prophets. We find two different types, one with a four-winged scarabæus, the other with a flying roll between the lines of the inscription, as in Zech. 5 : 1.[138] The former is clearly the older of the two, both because of the more archaic appearance of the pottery and because of its greater rarity in sites which were occupied down to the time of the Exile. These stamped jar-handles are of great chronological value, since they help to establish the fact that most of the

fortified towns of Judah were destroyed by the Chaldæans at the time of the Captivity, and not by
Sennacherib, or even by a later invader, as has frequently been supposed in the past.

Of even greater chronological value are two
stamped jar-handles found respectively in the second
and third campaigns. Both bear the same seal impression, which reads " Belonging to Eliakim steward
of Yôkîn." [139]   An identical inscribed handle was
found by Grant at Beth-shemesh in 1930, so that we
now have three examples, all impressed by the very
same seal, as shown by a minute comparison. *Yôkîn*
is a shortened form of the name of Joiachin, as was
first seen by Père Vincent, who examined the first
handle on the day of its discovery. Eliakim must
have been charged with the administration of the
personal property of Joiachin during the reign of
Zedekiah (597–87).[140]   As will be recalled, Joiakim
revolted against Nebuchadnezzar, but died just before
the Chaldæan invasion, or shortly afterwards. His
son and successor, Joiachin, a lad of eighteen, occupied the throne only three months (597), after
which he surrendered to the enemy, and was taken as
a prisoner to Babylon.[141] The people were anxious for
his return, since they considered him as the rightful
king, and his uncle Zedekiah as regent for him.[142]
Under such conditions, the latter could not have seized
his property with impunity, especially since David
had set a precedent three centuries before by leaving
the estate of Saul in the hands of Meribaal, for whom
Saul's own steward, Ziba, administered it.

The value of this seal impression is heightened by
the circumstances under which it was found. As we
have said, there were in some areas of A no fewer

than three superimposed phases of construction. The stamped handle in question was found in such an area, in the uppermost of the three phases of building. Moreover it here represents a very local phase of construction, under which continues the phase which all around this area comes to the top of the excavation. In other words, what was, in general, the latest phase of building is interrupted at this point by a reconstruction, which must, therefore, belong to the last years of the history of the town. The masonry of this reconstruction is very inferior, a fact which is all the more striking because of the uniformity of the masonry of late A as a whole. In other places in the A stratum we may also note that there was at the very last a period of decreased prosperity, when very poor repairs were made. Such a decline in prosperity began after the death of Josiah, when the land was swept by repeated invasions, followed by the imposition of heavy taxes. At the same time the stability of the state and the competence of its rulers declined, so that the country must have been rapidly impoverished. In these last years, to which we must date our seal impression, both for historical and for archæological reasons, the doom of Tell Beit Mirsim was sealed. Its fall probably occurred in 588, the year in which the last siege of Jerusalem began. How terrific the conflagration by which it was destroyed may have been can be gauged by the fact that limestone was calcined and slivered, while adobe was burned red; the ruins were saturated with free lime, which the seepage of water caused to adhere to pottery and other objects until they became coated with a tenacious crust of lime.

THE BIBLE IN THE LIGHT OF ARCHÆOLOGY

1. THE BEARING OF ARCHÆOLOGY ON BIBLICAL PROBLEMS

ARCHÆOLOGICAL research in Palestine and neighbouring lands during the past century has completely transformed our knowledge of the historical and literary background of the Bible. It no longer appears as an absolutely isolated monument of the past, as a phenomenon without relation to its environment. It now takes its place in a context which is becoming better known every year. Seen against the background of the ancient Near East, innumerable obscurities become clear, and we begin to comprehend the organic development of Hebrew society and culture. However, the uniqueness of the Bible, both as a masterpiece of literature and as a religious document, has not been lessened, and nothing tending to disturb the religious faith of Jew or Christian has been discovered.

As will be shown in the following pages, there has been a distinct gain to theology from this research. On the one hand, the excessive skepticism shown toward the Bible by important historical schools of the eighteenth and nineteenth centuries, certain phases of which still appear periodically, has been progressively discredited. Discovery after discovery has established the accuracy of innumerable details, and has brought increased recognition of the value of the Bible as a source of history. On the other hand, the theory of verbal inspiration—sometimes miscalled a doctrine —has been proved to be erroneous. The discovery that conceptions and practises evolve through many stages has led the leading Catholic and Protestant theologians to adopt a revised interpretation of the doctrine of progressive revelation, a line of defense behind which theology is secure from further encroachments on the part of the archæologist and the historian.

The most practical way in which to illustrate the importance of archæology for the better comprehension of the Bible is to select several outstanding problems of Hebrew history, and to discuss them in chronological order, in order to make their relation clearer. We shall, accordingly, choose the following topics for our discussion: the Age of the Patriarchs as described in Genesis; the Mosaic Law; the period of the Exile and the Restoration. It would hardly be advantageous, with the limited time at our disposal, to describe the innumerable archæological confirmations of the historical record of Joshua, Judges, Samuel, and Kings. A very interesting and important theme is that which deals with the new light on the social and economic background of the prophetic movement of the eighth and seventh centuries, but since we must select, let us choose the topics listed above. As will be seen, they are all storm-centers in the long struggle between Biblical critics, and there is no general agreement among scholars as to the interpretation of our data. However, recent archæological discoveries in Palestine and neighbouring lands speak with no uncertain voice, so that it is high time for the scholar who is in touch with them to express his views, even if they may sometimes appear rash.

2.   THE AGE OF THE PATRIARCHS IN THE LIGHT OF ARCHÆOLOGY

The orthodox critical attitude toward the traditions of the Patriarchs was summed up by the gifted founder of this school, Julius Wellhausen, in the following words: " From the patriarchal narratives it is impossible to obtain any historical information with regard to the Patriarchs; we can only learn something about the time in which the stories about them were first told by the Israelite people. This later period, with all its essential and superficial characteristics, was unintentionally projected back into hoary antiquity, and is reflected there like a transfigured mirage." [1] In other words, the account given in Genesis of the life of the Patriarchs is a faithful picture of the life of Israelites at the time when this account was composed, *i. e.*, according to the view of the dominant critical school, in the ninth and the eighth centuries B. C. The nomadic touches were derived, it is supposed, from the life of the Arab nomads of the day —or perhaps from the life of the Judæan nomadic tribes of the Negeb. Practically all of the Old Testament scholars of standing in Europe and America held these or similar views until very recently. Now, however, the situation is changing with the greatest rapidity, since the theory of Wellhausen will not bear the test of archæological examination.[2] The opposition to this theory began in the camp of Assyriology, where the gauntlet was thrown by Sayce, Hommel, and

Winckler,[3] but the methods employed by these scholars were so fanciful, and the knowledge of ancient Palestine (apart from the Bible) which then existed was so slight, that they were not taken seriously by their antagonists.

As an illustration of the changing attitude, let me call attention to the recent brochure by Professor Böhl of Leyden, *Das Zeitalter Abrahams* (Leipzig, 1930).[4] In this little book, Böhl, a successor of Kuenen, Wellhausen's lieutenant, maintains the essential historicity of the Patriarchs, and closes with the words: "Just as the Homeric Age stands at the beginning of Greek history, so does the Age of the Patriarchs in Israelite. Through the mist of ages we greet the figure of Abraham, whom Christians, Jews, and Mohammedans reverence as a ' friend of God ' and as the ' father of all who believe. ' " Another illustration is the monograph by Professor Alt of Leipzig on *Der Gott der Väter* (Stuttgart, 1929), in which the brilliant author shows that the patriarchal religion, as described in Genesis, is not an artificial construction of priestly historians of a later day, but actually reflects pre-Mosaic conditions: "Abraham, Isaac, and Jacob remain on the other side of Moses; but the lines which lead from their gods to the God of Israel have become distinct." [5] Shades of Wellhausen and Kuenen!

In Genesis the Patriarchs are portrayed as semi-nomadic, *i. e.,* as devoting themselves partly to sheep-raising and cattle-breeding, and partly to agriculture. They are, moreover, represented as wandering slowly about the country, but as having definite bases, to which they invariably return. They always wander about the hill-country or the extreme north of the Negeb, never on the coastal plains or in the desert.

Were this description of their life a late invention, we should have the greatest difficulty in finding an adequate explanation of its origin, since it does not agree at all with conditions in any part of Palestine in the Iron Age, to say nothing of Early Iron II. Wellhausen and his followers did not even recognize the difficulty, because of their ignorance of modern Palestine and adjoining lands. The Arabs of to-day distinguish sharply between *Fellāḥîn,* " peasants," *'Arab,* " semi-nomadic Arabs," and *Bédū,* " nomads." All the Arabs who are entirely sedentary are called *fellāḥîn,* even if they only remain in their village during two or three months of the year, as at Dûrā and Beit Feddjâr.[6] If, however, they live entirely, or almost entirely in tents, and yet do not move outside of their own restricted district, which they till regularly, they are *'Arab,* like the 'Azâzmeh around Beersheba, or the Ta'âmreh about Tekoa. True nomads, who despise agriculture, and preserve the noble traditions—and poverty—of the desert, like the 'Anezeh and the Ruwâlā, are called *Bédū, i. e.,* Bedouins. It is clear that the Patriarchs come under the category of *'Arab.* Yet they do not correspond exactly to the *'Arab.* Their scope of wandering, which extends from Mesopotamia through Syria into central and southern Palestine, is much greater, and they wander between fortified towns and districts occupied by a purely sedentary population, engaging in trade relations with the latter. In the Early Iron Age there was no true analogy, since the Kenites were a very highly specialized group.[7]

Here archæology provides the necessary explanation. In the Middle and Late Bronze Ages the hill-country was still but sparsely peopled, and almost the entire sedentary population occupied the coastal plains, Esdraelon, and the Jordan Valley. The plains and broad valleys were dotted with towns, as shown by the innumerable mounds which remain to mark them. Occupation in these regions was considerably denser than it was in the Iron Age, or than it is to-day. A century ago the plains and the Jordan Valley were largely occupied by '*Arab,* while the sedentary population (outside of Gaza, Jaffa, Acre, etc.) was almost entirely in the hill-country—a curious reversal of conditions in the Bronze Age. The mountains of Palestine were then heavily forested on the watershed ridge and the western slopes, so that little space was left for agriculture. Moreover, cisterns had not then come into general use, so there were no settlements except where good springs were located just under a low hill, suitable for defense, with meadows or broader valleys near by, to ensure a supply of food. Between these fortified towns, most of which were situated on the watershed ridge or near it, there was ample room for semi-nomadic tribes, which have left abundant traces of their existence in cemeteries containing Middle and Late Bronze pottery, but too far from towns to have been employed by the sedentary population. In Genesis also we are told that the Patriarchs buried their dead in the Cave of Machpelah, following the customs of the settled inhabitants of the land. The Amarna Tablets call these semi-nomadic people the Khabiru, a name which is probably to be identified with Biblical " Hebrew." [8] The Khabiru correspond closely, at all events, to the Hebrews of the patriarchal period in many important respects: in their independence of towns, in their geographical localization in Palestine, in their warlike spirit. At least once we learn of a Canaanite coalition to resist their encroachments.

According to the Wellhausen school, the association of certain towns with the history of the Patriarchs is due simply to the fact that cult-legends relating to them were attached to these places in much later times. If we consider the situation in the light of the topographical and archæological researches of the past few years, we will discover the interesting fact that practically every town mentioned in the narratives of the Patriarchs was in existence in the Middle Bronze Age. Examples are Shechem,[9] Bethel,[10] Ai,[11] Jerusalem (Salem),[12] Gerar,[13] Dothan,[14] Beersheba.[15] Aside from the case of the Cities of the Plain, which we shall take up presently, there is only Hebron whose existence at that time cannot be established archæologically.[16] From its situation in an extremely fruitful and well-watered valley, there can be no reasonable doubt that Hebron was occupied at a very early date, especially since neighbouring cemeteries, plundered by the Arabs, have yielded a great many Middle Bronze remains.[17] If the patriarchal stories were first told as we have them in the Iron Age, we should expect to find references to Israelite settlements like Mizpah and Gibeah, etc., etc.

The story of the Cities of the Plain is still obscure in many respects. However, the tradition that the Plain of the Jordan, where these towns were located, was exceedingly fruitful and well peopled at the time of the first entrance of the Hebrews into the country, but that it was shortly afterwards abandoned, is absolutely in accord with the archæological facts. As recently as 1928 the famous ancient historian, Eduard Meyer, knowing nothing of the researches of the

American School in the Jordan Valley, was able to say of this region in the fifteenth century B. C.: "Absolutely barren lay also the Jordan Valley south of Beth-shan and Pella, burning hot between the mountain walls on both sides, through which it cut its broad and deep way. . . . Here the attempt was never made to utilize the soil and to make it productive by systematic irrigation, as was done in the Nile Valley under essentially the same conditions(!)." [18] From about 1922 on, the writer has carried on explorations in the Jordan Valley, culminating in an expedition undertaken with the coöperation of Dr. M. G. Kyle in 1924, for the purpose of studying the archæological remains of the southern Ghôr (Jordan Valley). [19] These researches and those of Père Mallon and other scholars [20] have proved that the most prosperous period of the history of this valley was in the Early Bronze Age, and that the density of its occupation gradually declined until it reached its lowest point in the Early Iron II, after the tenth century B. C. Except in the Turkish period (before the Jewish colonization began toward the end of the nineteenth century A. D.) this was the age of least occupation in the valley's history. Yet we are asked by some to believe that the traditions of its pristine fertility arose in the Iron Age!

In 1924 we obtained an entirely satisfactory solution of the problem of the situation of the five Cities of the Plain, Sodom, Gomorrah, Admah, Zeboim, and Zoar. It is true that an attempt has recently been made to establish another solution, but the archæological basis of this effort is as fragile as its documentary support. [21] At the southeastern end of the Dead Sea there are several fine streams of

fresh water, which form fruitful oases, the only ones
on the shores of the Dead Sea, aside from Engedi,
on the west side, with an absolutely certain identification.   A search through these oases and the environs
failed to yield any remains antedating the Roman
period, except at Bâb ed-Drâ', of which more presently.   However, the shallow southern basin of the
Dead Sea has been encroaching on its shores steadily
for the past century, during which its area has increased fully one-third, according to the best calcula-
tion.[22]   The encroachment of the deadly salt water
has forced the irrigated oases upstream toward the
foot of the wall of mountains on the east.   One oasis,
which was occupied in Byzantine times, has been almost completely swallowed up, since there is no room
left for irrigation at this point.   In Roman, Byzantine,
and Arabic times there was a little city, which still
bore the ancient name Zoar, near the Seil el-Qurâḥi,
at the southern end of the sea; its site, which we examined and sounded, exhibits no traces of a pre-
Christian occupation.   It follows, of course, since the
situation of Zoar in the extreme south is testified by
several Biblical passages, that the later site, at the
foot of the hills, lies upstream from the Biblical site,
and that the latter, like the former oasis of the Seil
en-Numeirah, has been buried by the advancing waters
of the Dead Sea.   These oases which we have mentioned must have been occupied by a sedentary
population in the Bronze Age, since every similar
oasis, where irrigation is possible, in the Jordan Valley north of the Dead Sea, has its *tell* to mark the
site of a Bronze Age town.   More than one town in
the same stream-basin was impossible, since the con-
flict over water-rights would effectually eliminate any

attempt at competition in a very short time. Even if the curious coincidence of the five Cities of the Plain with five modern oases in this region should be accidental, we are, therefore, quite justified in placing them here, and in supposing that their sites have long since been covered by the Dead Sea, though they may have been exposed to view until post-Biblical times.

The archæological proof of the existence of a sedentary population in this district was obtained by the discovery of Bâb ed-Drâ', a great fortified enclosure, partly surrounded by a settlement of booths (marked by enclosures and hearths) and cemeteries, with a prostrate alignment of stone pillars (*maṣṣebôth*), evidently representing a high-place. Vast quantities of potsherds, flint artifacts, and other remains fixed the date between the middle of the third millennium (Early Bronze II), at the earliest, and the nineteenth century B. C., at the latest. Some of the pieces belong unmistakably to the transition from Early to Middle Bronze, which we cannot, however, date with precision as yet. The character of the fortified enclosure, the remains of houses found in it, and the remains of booths (not tents) found outside of it prove that the installation belonged to a sedentary population. It is most emphatically not a city, but rather a temporary encampment, like Gilgal, or perhaps rather like the somewhat shadowy Baal-peor of Moab. Since the plain of Bâb ed-Drâ' is not suitable for cultivation, and is high above the gorge of the Seil ed-Drâ', it would in any case be a very unsatisfactory place for a town. As a festival site for the inhabitants of the oases below it is admirable, since it is situated on the first convenient rise of terrain above the central oasis of el-Mezra'ah, some five hundred feet above the level of the Dead Sea.

The fact that occupation ended here abruptly at the beginning of the second millennium, not later than 1800 B. C. at the outside,[23] is unquestionably a strong argument for the historicity of the tradition that the towns of this district were destroyed in a natural cataclysm about this time. It would also set an upper limit for the date of Abraham, or at least of his general age. It might, of course, permit a lower date, since we have no proof that Bâb ed-Drâ' was abandoned because of the cataclysm described in Genesis; it may have been deserted previously, for some reason which escapes our control. However, it does suggest very strongly that the date of Abraham cannot be placed earlier than the nineteenth century B. C.

In the patriarchal stories as they are handed down to us we have several very enigmatic episodes and references, which were probably just as obscure to the Israelite of the period of the Divided Monarchy to which these narratives belong, in their present form, as they are to most Biblical scholars of to-day. For their interpretation we must turn to recent archæological discoveries in Mesopotamia. In 1925 E. Chiera, then field director of the American School of Oriental Research in Baghdad, began excavations at Yorghan Tepe near Kirkûk in southeastern Assyria, excavations which have been continued with little interruption until the present year (1931), in collaboration with Harvard University.[24] Among other important discoveries were several thousand cuneiform tablets from the fifteenth and fourteenth centuries B. C. The city bore the name Nuzi, and was occupied by a Hurrian population, belonging to the same ethnic group, as shown by the evidence of proper names, etc., as that which then prevailed in all northern Mesopotamia, as well as in eastern Syria. A large proportion of the documents found bore the heading " tablet of adoption (to sonship, Assyr. *marûtu*)." There was an old principle of civil law among the Hurrians which forbade the alienation of inherited land—an illustration of the powerful operation of family solidarity. In practise, however, a way was found by which this prohibition could be nullified. Wealthy creditors had themselves legally adopted by the debtor, and acquired immediate possession of his land by this simple expedient. The debtor " foster-parents " received a small compensation, and became tenants of their creditors—*i. e.,* virtually serfs. At an earlier period, however, the principle of adoption worked differently, and was then naturally connected with religious ideas with regard to the importance of having the family estate (and the care of the ancestor's funerary rites) kept in the hands of a legal heir. This practise, which fell into disuse long before the Iron Age, is evidently the reason for the hitherto obscure adoption of Eliezer by Abraham, before the birth of Isaac.[25]

A much more striking, though not so fundamental parallel has been pointed out by Sidney Smith and C. J. Gadd, in the latter's edition of a group of Kirkûk texts.[26] In a tablet of adoption a certain Nashwa declares that he has adopted Wullu, son of Pukhishenni (the head of a wealthy family of Nuzi). Wullu (the creditor) states that he will provide Nashwa with food and clothing, and will see that he is properly buried. Then we read: " If Nashwa has a son, he shall divide (the property) equally with

Wullu, and the son of Nashwa shall take Nashwa's gods; but if Nashwa has no son, Wullu shall take Nashwa's gods." In other words: the legitimate heir has a prior right to possession of the household gods, and the adoptive heir cannot take them unless there is no legitimate heir. Possession of the gods was naturally believed to include divine protection of the land of the family to whom the gods in question were attached. The purpose of the document, to legalize an act of oppression, does not affect its legal form, which goes back to an earlier day, when adoption had another basis (see above). This tablet enables us to understand the meaning of the puzzling episode in Genesis (31: 19–35), which describes Jacob's flight from Laban and Rachel's successful theft of the household gods (teraphim). As will be recalled, Laban was more exercised by the loss of the gods than by the flight of his daughters and their husband, with all the accumulated wealth of cattle. The primary motivation of this story was evidently that Rachel stole the gods in order to assure the inheritance to her husband.

Among modern Biblical scholars there has been hardly one to accept the traditional Hebrew account of Abraham's Mesopotamian origin, from Ur [27] and Harran. And yet there is very strong evidence in support of the tradition. In the first place, it cannot be accidental that the names of the clan-ancestors who figure in the genealogy of Abraham [28] occur in Assyrian times as place-names (*i. e.,* old names of clans) in the region of Harran: *e. g.,* Terah, Nahor, Serug.[29] The name Arphaxad is also probably Mesopotamian.[30] Nor can we overlook the increasing probability that some of the cosmogonic stories of Genesis came from

Northern Mesopotamia. The view that these stories were borrowed from Mesopotamia at a late date has now been given up by all competent scholars. They may, of course, have been adopted by the Hebrews from a secondary Palestinian source, as is probably held now by most scholars. Against it is, however, the fact which we have already stressed, that the pre-Israelite religion of Canaan was very different in many respects from the paganism of Israel after the Conquest, which contained elements borrowed at a later date from purely Iron Age cultures. It is most unlikely that the Hebrews would have borrowed such stories as that of the Flood from their neighbours after their settlement in Palestine. The divergence of the J and E recensions is alone sufficient to establish the antiquity of the common original, which was already distinctly Israelite. A Hurrian source for the name Noah has recently been suggested.[31] However this may be, the fact that the ark grounded in the Armenian mountains (*Ararat*=*Urartu*) indicates a North Mesopotamian source, since the Babylonians sought their mountain of the ark in the Zagros, which lay north of Babylonia.[32] Elsewhere, also, sacred mountains are generally in the north.[33] If the Canaanites possessed a Flood-story, we may safely suppose that Lebanon or Hermon played the corresponding rôle. The story of Paradise, which locates the Garden of Bliss at the source of the Euphrates and Tigris, and employs a northwestern Mesopotamian place-name to describe it, is clearly derived from the same region.[34]

We have left the discussion of Genesis XIV to the last, since it does not belong to the documents J and E, and its relation to P is extremely obscure. It is in any case a prose abstract of a poetic narrative, as is proved by numerous snatches of verse, which have not been eliminated from the prose version as carefully as was usually the case (see below).[35] However, the very obviousness of its poetic origin gives us a guarantee of the age and the essential accuracy of the names, which are always better transmitted in poetic saga than in prose narrative. The subject has been elaborately discussed by the writer and by F. M. Th. Böhl, to whose treatments we may refer.[36] Suffice it to say here that our main contentions hold just as firmly as ever. The events of this chapter have nothing to do with Hammurabi of Babylon, but must be dated considerably later; Shinar (originally pronounced *Shanghar*) is a country in central Mesopotamia, and is not Babylonia. Whether the writer's view that the invasion of Chedorlaomer took place in the eighteenth century is correct or not, the episode must be dated in the unsettled age between the fall of the First Dynasty of Babylon (cir. 1806 B. C.)[37] and the Egyptian conquest of Palestine and Syria in the sixteenth century. There are two very remarkable facts about this chapter. First is its use of archaic words and place-names, occurring nowhere else in the Bible. Since this has been discussed by other scholars, I shall limit myself to two illustrations, both new. The retainers of Abraham are called by the name *hanîkîm* (Gen. 14: 14). In a cuneiform letter found by Sellin at Taanach in Palestine, and dating from the fifteenth century or earlier,[38] the same word appears in the form *hanakû,* pointing to a correct vocalization *hanakîm* in Genesis. But the word is Egyptian, and is used in Egyptian texts dating from about 2000 B. C. for the retainers of Palestinian chieftains.[39] In later times the word became disused. The second illustration is the place-name Ham, mentioned 14:5. Several years ago the writer and Professor Steuernagel of Breslau independently saw that this Ham might be identical with a modern place of the same name in eastern Gilead.[40]   In 1929 Professor Jirku of Breslau and the writer undertook to investigate the antiquities of Ham, and immediately discovered the presence there of a small, but very ancient, mound going back to the Bronze Age.[41]   The name also occurs in the list of towns conquered by Pharaoh Tuthmosis III in Palestine, about 1480 B. C.

It is, of course, improbable that a poetic saga of such great age can be taken as literal history throughout; there are sufficient indications in the chapter of its popular origin.   However, the underlying account of the campaign waged by the Eastern kings appears to be historical.   This account represents the invading host as marching down from Haurân through eastern Gilead and Moab to the southeastern part of Palestine. Formerly the writer considered this extraordinary line of march as being the best proof of the essentially legendary character of the narrative.   In 1929, however, he discovered a line of Early and Middle Bronze Age mounds, some of great size, running down along the eastern edge of Gilead, between the desert and the forests of Gilead.[42]   Moreover, the cities of Haurân (Bashan) with which the account of the campaign opens, Ashtaroth and Karnaim, were both occupied in this period, as shown by archæological examination of their sites.   The same is true of eastern Moab, where the writer discovered an Early-Middle Bronze city at Ader in 1924.[43]   This route, called " The Way of the King " in later Israelite tradition, does not appear to have ever been employed by invading armies in the Iron Age. Some inkling of the reason which led the Eastern army down into the region of Seir, far south of the Dead Sea, may perhaps be obtained from the fact that there were extensive and important deposits of copper, manganese (used for *kuhl*—see above), and other minerals in Seir and Midian.[44] From the still only partially deciphered inscriptions of Sinai we know how actively the natives of this region engaged in mining during this very age (about the eighteenth century B. C.).

The story of Joseph falls into a somewhat different category. Since the story was so popular, and dealt with Egypt, the temptation for Israelite scribes who were acquainted with Egyptian and with life in Egypt to revise the names and details was irresistible. It has long since been pointed out by Egyptologists that the Egyptian names in the story are late, and cannot be dated before the tenth century, at the earliest.[45] To conclude that the story of Joseph is therefore legendary, or even a romantic invention of later times, is, however, just as unreasonable as it would be to deduce from the still later Egyptianizing of names in the Septuagintal version that the Joseph story was compiled by the Alexandrian scribes.[46] There can be no doubt whatever that the Hebrews played an important rôle in Egypt during the Hyksos period, as is shown by the names of *Ya'qob-har*, belonging to a dynast,[47] and *Ḥûr*, name of the chancellor of one of the Hyksos monarchs.[48] As is well known, the close connection between the Hyksos and the Age of the Patriarchs is reflected by an antiquarian gloss in Numbers, stating that Hebron was built seven years before Tanis in Egypt.[49] The Era of Tanis represents the Hyksos restoration of the city, soon after their invasion, as has recently been shown anew by Sethe.[50] The writer has long believed that the number 430 in Ex. 12:40–1 follows the Era of Tanis, since it does not seem to be a round number; should this prove correct, we should have a definite date for the Exodus, early in the thirteenth century, with the Conquest a generation later.

The extraordinary accuracy of the narratives of the Patriarchs, when tested by our rapidly accumulating material, is no longer surprising if we consider two parallels. The first is that of the Homeric Epics, particularly the Iliad.[51] For the century preceding the discovery of the Mycenæan Age of Greece, most serious scholars had considered it as either mythical or as reflecting conditions in the early part of the first millennium. With the rapid increase of archæological data it has become quite impossible to maintain this view any longer. The Iliad proves to reflect most faithfully, as a rule, conditions at the end of the Late Bronze Age, that is, of the period which it purports to describe. There are, of course, anachronisms: iron is mentioned a little too frequently, and the dead are cremated instead of buried; but, in general, these exceptions to the prevailing historical accuracy of cultural detail are so few as to bring out the latter with all the more force. The Iliad describes events which transpired in the thirteenth and twelfth centuries; it was compiled from older epic lays about the tenth or the ninth century, and was put into written form in the sixth century, more than six hundred years after the fall of Troy. Another parallel is furnished by the Rig Veda, whose history is much more obscure, but in some ways even more striking. There is now general agreement that the Rig Veda came into existence between 1800 and 1200 B. C., that is, after the Aryan invasion of India, but in the Bronze Age.[52] When its hymns were collected and the canon was fixed is a more elusive question. It cannot, in any event, have been reduced to writing until the Greek period, *i. e.,* after the third century B. C. In its case we must allow at least a millennium between the original composition of the hymns and their earliest written form.

In view of these parallels it is difficult to see anything very remarkable in the conclusion which has been forced upon us by recent archæological discoveries, that the saga of the Patriarchs is essentially historical. However, it follows that this saga was transmitted in poetic form, since prose narratives are never handed down very long by oral instrumentality. We have seen that Genesis XIV requires a poetic prototype. Such poetic prototypes of prose narratives are preserved in a number of cases; the best known is the Song of Deborah.[53] Careful perusal of the prose narratives of the Hexateuch shows numerous indications of their original poetic basis, which appears again and again in poetic quotations, in verses placed in the mouths of characters, in highly poetic similes, and in archaic expressions which betray their origin by their rhythmic swing.[54] The Song of Miriam (Exodus XV) and the poems of Balaam probably are examples of compositions in verse which preceded the prose compilations which we possess, though it is true that they were considerably expanded in later times. No one can without obvious prejudice maintain that the superb couplet:

Sing to the Lord,   For greatly exalted is He,
Horse and chariot [55]   He hath cast into the sea

is long posterior to the Exodus. Nor can one suppose without severe mental strain that the passage in the story of Balaam, Num. 24:24, describing the coming of invaders from the direction of the Ægean and their subjugation of the Hebrews, dates from long after the period of the Philistine invasion.[56]

As now recognized by the overwhelming majority of scholars, both those who belong to the Wellhausen school and those who are not members of this group, the narratives of the Hexateuch must be assigned, in general, to two different documents, called J and E (i. e., the " Jahwistic " or Yahwistic, otherwise called the Judæan, and the Elohistic, otherwise the Ephraimite). P does not play any great rôle in the narratives, so we may disregard it here. The written composition of these documents is generally dated between the ninth century (J) and the eighth (E), though Sellin, for instance, prefers to date J in the tenth and E at the end of the eighth. Kittel and others have stressed the extraordinary parallelism between the narratives of J and E, which agree altogether too closely for two entirely independent bodies of late tradition.[57] We must suppose that they both go back to a common source, or a common group of sources, which in any case antedate the time of David. Now Böhl has recently emphasized the fact that the patriarchal stories of Genesis belong to a greater literary whole.[58] The inner unity is, he observes, unmistakable, despite the presence of various documents and sources. The fundamental conception is developed in the story of the Patriarchs with a logical coherence which is rarely found in other ancient literature. Moreover, the unity of artistic conception and execution is equally clear. Even without the aid of delineations of character the figures of Abraham, of Isaac, and of Jacob appear before us in all their humanity, yet with a clearness of outline that not even the composite structure of our text can materially affect.   Such unity and harmony remain inexplicable unless we assume that they are due to a great poetic genius, who cast the poetic sagas of the Patriarchs into a single saga.   Similarly, there must have been an early saga of the Exodus and a saga—or sagas—of the Conquest of Canaan.   This group of sagas became standard throughout Israel, and was perhaps officially sanctioned by the priesthood of Shiloh.   After the Division of the Kingdom—perhaps after the fall of Shiloh, some century and a quarter before—the sagas became differentiated into a northern and a southern group, which continued to be transmitted orally.   In the course of time variations were introduced, part of which came probably from local sources, as is certainly true of the traditions with regard to places and details of the Israelite Conquest.   Finally, after this double period of oral transmission, these two groups of sagas were reduced to writing in the late eighth century (J) and early seventh (E).[59]

Kittel and others have stressed the significance of this double transmission for our reconstruction of the underlying history.   Events which are attested by J and E alike belong certainly to the great saga cycle of the time of the Judges.   But since, in compiling JE in the seventh century, the scribes were careful not to repeat stories and details which did not differ appreciably in the two accounts, we have no right to suspect the originality of singular elements of J and E. Knowing the extraordinary care with which ancient scribes avoided the introduction of unwarranted innovations into their compilations, we must always assume that such a singular element came either from one of the documents (having been accidentally lost in the other), or from an outside (but perhaps equally old) source.

The original sagas of the Patriarchs naturally went back into the post-patriarchal age, just as the sagas from which the Iliad was compiled belong to the two centuries after the Fall of Troy. An equally good parallel may be drawn from the study of the sources of the Nibelungenlied.[60] That they were partly, perhaps mainly handed down in Palestine, rather than in Egypt,[61] may be regarded as practically certain, since it is now quite certain that a large part, perhaps more than half of the Hebrew people remained in Palestine, and did not enter Egypt at all.[62] Their extreme antiquity explains why they contain so many elements derived from the common stock of ancient Oriental folklore. To have shown this is the merit of the late Hugo Winckler, who unfortunately spoiled his work by introducing the wildest astral speculations into it. The fact that there are so many elements of folklore, especially in the stories of Jacob and of Joseph, does not injure the historical and pedagogical value of Genesis. Quite the contrary—it enhances its value in both respects. We must remember that the transmission of oral and written documents or narratives is conditioned by a different set of laws in each case. The laws governing the transmission of written documents are well known; every student knows something about them. Written documents are compiled by the dovetailing together of different sources, as in the work of the Chronicler, or in the writings of ancient and mediæval chronographers. They are ed-

ited or redacted, as in the case of the documents from
the Northern Kingdom, which were put into Biblical
Hebrew (the language of Jerusalem), or the work of
the Masoretes in establishing a uniform Hebrew text
and pointing it according to their interpretation of it.
They are copied over a long period of time, during
which all sorts of errors (belonging to a number of
well-understood types) creep into the text. They are
translated, in which case new errors creep in, as every
tyro knows from experience.

In the same way, the transmission of oral tradition is bound by its form. If the latter is poetic,
the tradition persists with sometimes most incredible
tenacity. If the tradition is prose, it seldom lasts
more than three or four generations, even among
the Semites (e. g., modern Arabs). Moreover,
nearly all tradition has a short period of prose transmission before it is put into verse. During this
period it is adjusted to the requirements of the popular mind by being classified into various standard
categories, which necessarily have a folkloristic background. Since there was no clear demarcation in
antiquity between what we now call myth and folklore,
we must not be surprised to find mythical elements in
the stories of the Patriarchs—or perhaps we should
say, elements of a mythical—i. e., folkloristic—origin.
The nature of the framework which was chosen de-
pended upon the suggestive power of the historical
events which underlie each saga. For example, the
Joseph story has been very strongly influenced by the
cycle of folklore which revolved around the figures of
certain popular gods of fertility, such as Bitis, Osiris,
and Adonis.[63] Yet it does not follow that Joseph is
a myth, or that the events narrated of him are fic-

titious. On the contrary, it is precisely because the traditional history of Joseph bore such a striking similarity to the mythical careers of popular gods of fertility, which became heroes of folklore at a very early date, that the fusion of history with folklore was produced. Oral tradition inevitably implies the accretion of elements from folklore, as illustrated by the earliest historical memories of every ancient people, as well as by the myths and legends which have gathered around the name of every notable monarch or sage, from Sargon of Accad and Imuthes to Akhiqar and Alexander.[64] A historical person may thus be surrounded in time with the borrowed aureole of a god, as in the case of Semiramis, whose later story became almost entirely mythical, though she was once queen-regent of Assyria (in the ninth century B. C.).[65] We are learning that oral history and folklore are naturally complementary, and that historical saga is invariably composed of nuclei of fact clad in garments of folklore. As a matter of fact, most actual occurrences of sufficiently remarkable nature to form soil for the growth of saga are characterized from the beginning by extraordinary coincidences and curious plots which inevitably attract wandering folklore motives.

A moment's consideration should convince anyone that we are very fortunate indeed in the oral transmission of the earliest history of the Hebrews. Were it possible for us to have a written record of the external events of that period—since an account of the internal development of character by an eye-witness is inconceivable in such a remote age—we should have a very dull and pedagogically useless record of clan and tribal history. Instead we have an ample historical basis, on which is constructed a stately edifice of saga. Psychologically this saga, which has enshrined for us the accumulated wisdom and experience of the ancient Orient, collected and sifted during many thousands of years, and has eliminated all barbarous and obviously pagan elements, is truer history than the record of clan movements and wars would be. The one enables us to enter into the life and innermost heart of Israel; the other would be useful to a political historian, and all but useless to the teacher. It is the pedagogical value of sagas that determines their success, in the last analysis. Happily we have both political history and psychological history; we are able to see our own trials and aspirations portrayed on heroic canvas at the same time that we can follow the religious and political evolution of the Chosen People.

3. THE LAW OF MOSES

The second great question which we have set ourselves to elucidate, so far as possible, from the data of archæology is the Mosaic Law. We cannot do more than to touch so vast and complicated a subject as the age and the nature of the Torah in a few brief pages. The Wellhausen school maintains that the civil and religious legislation of the Pentateuch belongs to three different strata, published in the following order: J, E, and the Book of the Covenant (Ex. 20: 22–23: 33), before the seventh century; Deuteronomy (D), B. C. 621; the Priestly Code (P, which includes part of Exodus, all of Leviticus, and part of Numbers), which dates from the time of Ezra (B. C. 450), though composed during and after the Babylonian Exile. Wellhausen himself and some of his followers recognized the antiquity of some of this legislation, part of which Wellhausen thought to be of pre-Mosaic origin, though he did not attempt to specify instances.[66] Most of the members of this great school have, however, rather carelessly assumed that the laws and regulations belong as a whole to the period when the codes were published, though they may admit the greater antiquity of certain prescriptions.

A change began to be felt among scholars after the publication of the famous Code of Hammurabi in 1902.[67] It became gradually understood that certain Hebrew laws stood in closer relation to the Code of Hammurabi than they did to the legal practice of Assyria and Babylonia in the first millennium B. C., as it is known from cuneiform business documents. Yet the Code of Hammurabi dates from the twentieth century B. C., and incorporates much older Sumerian material, as is now known, thanks to the discovery and publication of numerous extracts from Sumerian collections of laws, belonging to the third millennium. The publication in 1920 of the Assyrian code,[68] from about the twelfth century B. C. (the date is uncertain), followed in 1921 by that of a Hittite code [69] from the thirteenth century, but also incorporating much older material, has greatly extended our scope of comparison. A galaxy of brilliant European jurists is now engaged in comparative study of this rich material, which is enormously extended by the steady stream of contract tablets from all parts of Western Asia which are being discovered every year. It is sufficient to mention the names of Cuq, Kohler, Koschaker, Eisser, San Nicoló to illustrate the vast new field which is being opened up to students of social and economic history, as well as to Biblical scholars. Our knowledge of ancient Oriental religious legislation is also being extended vastly by new discoveries and publications of Babylonian, Assyrian, Hittite, and South Arabian documents, quite aside from the cuneiform, South Arabian, Phœnician and Egyptian inscriptions already known before the War. Virtually none of this material was accessible when Wellhausen wrote his epoch-making works, so it is not surprising that the latter now prove to be antiquated.

In 1921 Dussaud showed which way the wind blew by publishing a book in which he undertook to demonstrate the Canaanite origin of Israelite sacrificial ritual.[70] Jirku has followed with several less ambitious attempts to establish the relative chronology of certain types of Pentateuchal laws, in imitation of the methods being employed by Assyriologists and students of comparative law in their study of the cuneiform laws.[71] Others are following their example, so we may expect to see a great display of activity in this important field during the next decade. We shall not attempt to treat our subject from this angle, but rather from the standpoint of the Palestinian archæologist. A few observations may be permitted us before we pass on to the latter mode of approach. Dussaud's attempt to prove the dependence of Israelite sacrificial ritual upon Canaanite is undoubtedly correct to a certain extent. Israelites and Canaanites, both speaking Hebrew, and sharing a common external civilization, must be expected to use somewhat the same technical expressions, and to employ similar modes of slaughter, etc. However, it does not follow that the Israelites were necessarily heirs of the sacrificial practice of the Canaanites whom they displaced. We have seen in chapter II that the religious customs of the Israelite period (B and A) were different from those of the preceding Canaanite age, and that new pagan influences came from outside and were not (as a rule) inherited from the older Canaanite inhabitants of the district. We must, therefore, reckon partly with a common stock of beliefs and usages which were inherited by Hebrews and Canaanites from a common source, and partly with later borrowing from the Canaanites (Phœnicians) of the Iron Age, such as all admit to have taken place in the construction and furnishing of the Temple in the tenth century B. C.[72]

The publication of Deuteronomy in 621 B. C. is a fixed date in the uncertain field of Torah chronology; nearly all scholars adopt it, with more or less reservation with regard to the bearing of this fact upon the age of different parts of the book. However, a careful perusal of it in the light of chapter II will certainly convince most students that Deuteronomy sounds curiously archaic to have been written as a whole in the late seventh century B. C. On the other hand, it represents quite another period from that reflected by JE, since there is no trace (except in the historical introduction and in other similar reminiscences scattered through the book) of the nomadic or semi-nomadic period of Hebrew life. The civil code presupposed by Deuteronomy belongs to a stage before the development of the royal power, before the great commercial expansion of the eighth and seventh centuries, and consequently before the collapse of the ancient tribal and clan organization, which was gradually replaced during the royal period by a system of administrative districts and trade-guilds. Officials are still chosen locally, instead of being royal appointees (cf. 16:18, 17:9; 25:1-3 is ambiguous). On the other hand, as already observed, Deuteronomy is clearly younger than the period of the Judges. Quite aside from the passage referring to the monarchy (17:14-17), which belongs to about the ninth century,[73] and from the Blessing of Moses, belonging to about the same time,[74] there are clear archæological indications of a later date. Iron is mentioned a number of times (the best cases are 8:9, 27:5, 33:25). In 8:9, moreover, there is evidently a reference to the iron mines of Lebanon, just as the allusion to copper implies knowledge of the copper mines of Edom.[75] These iron mines cannot have been worked before the tenth century, at the earliest, since the Philistines could not have maintained their monopoly down to the time of Saul if iron had been conveniently accessible in a region outside of their control. The frequent references to writing in Deuteronomy point in the same direction; writing was certainly not employed in such cases as divorce contracts (24:1-4) before the monarchy. It is not our purpose to enter into the vexed problem of the unity or composite origin of the book; in our judgment it was written down, substantially as a unit, in the ninth century B. C., and was edited in the reign of Josiah or later. The North-Israelite origin of Deuteronomy, defended by Welch, Gressmann, and others [76] seems clear; the language does not help us, since it has in any case been put into the dialect of Jerusalem (classical Hebrew), so that northern peculiarities have been effaced. The most natural explanation is that Deuteronomy represents a selection from the religious and family legislation of the region of Shechem, in so far as it was believed in the ninth century B. C. to go back to Moses. It is probable that Shechem followed Shiloh as the cult-center of the Joseph tribes, and that the famous passage concerning the unification of cult in one place (12 : 8 ff., compared with 11 : 30) was originally intended to uphold the position of Shechem (following Shiloh).[77] The passage is certainly too vague to represent an original composition of the time of Josiah, for the purpose of ensuring Jerusalem a unique position as a cult-center.

Morgenstern has lately maintained the same general date for the Book of the Covenant, the nucleus of which he assigns to the reign of Asa, while its publication he refers to the Northern Kingdom, in the reign of Jehu, about 842 (841) B. C.[78] His view is very attractive; its rather archaic appearance would be due partly to the fact that the Book of the Covenant contains very old material, and partly to the absence of the revision which has given the cult legislation of Deuteronomy so modern an appearance in various respects.

The writer believes that there is a general similarity between the origin and transmission of the Torah in Israel and of the Ḥadîth in Islam. The latter is an expression meaning primarily " communication," and is applied by Moslems to a traditional saying or act of the Prophet, as well as to the entire corpus of such traditional records. These traditions are supposed to have been preserved in the memories of the companions of the Prophet, and to have been transmitted orally through the instrumentality of a chain of transmitters. The validity of each tradition depends in theory upon the reliability of the weakest link of the chain. In fact, the principal difference between the mode of transmission of the Ḥadîth and that of the

Torah, if our view is correct, is precisely the absence of the *isnâd* (chain of tradition) in the latter case. In the third century of the Hegira, written collections of the *Hadîth* began to be made, but by this time most of the accepted traditions were quite certainly apocryphal. The invention of new traditions was often due to the emergence of new conditions and problems, for which neither the Qurân nor the older traditions offered any solutions. In many cases, as Lammens has shown, new *hadîths* were circulated for the purpose of bolstering political pretensions. In many cases, again, traditions arose through misunderstanding, and sayings or acts were attributed to Mohammed which really belonged to someone else. It must be emphasized, however, that the accepted *Hadîth* was always believed to represent the very words and deeds of the Prophet, and that the collectors and editors of the corpus acted in perfect good faith.

Similarly, we may safely suppose that the collection of the sayings and deeds of Moses began in the second and third centuries after his death, and passed through somewhat the same vicissitudes as the collection of early Hebrew sagas, described above. JE (including such documents as the Book of the Covenant) represents the main stream of this tradition, while D may form a branch of the stream which separated from it at an early date, and had a complex history of its own thereafter. P, we believe, consists of the official tradition current in priestly circles of Jerusalem at the beginning of the Exile. Though the latest in date, it consciously and successfully endeavours to supplement the publication of JED by adding numerous details about the cult of the Mosaic period, and by bringing the description of Mosaic legislation up to date. We are not directly interested here in its contributions to the knowledge of early Hebrew history. The compilers of the P material possessed old oral and written sources which give it a very great value. It is quite true that some of this material was misunderstood, and does not belong in its present context. A case in point is the two census lists of Israel given by P in Num. 1 and 26, the first of which purports to be the enumeration made by Moses directly after the Exodus, while the latter is given as the result of an enumeration made after the forty years in the wilderness. The writer has pointed out elsewhere that a few simple transpositions and alterations of digits produce an identity between nearly all the census numbers of the respective tribes in the two enumerations.[79] This result proves that the two lists of tribal population are variants of one and the same original census list, which is probably that of the Davidic census, since no other enumeration of the entire population is recorded during the period of the United Monarchy, the only time when it could possibly have been made. It was shown that the numbers are precisely what we should expect in the time of David, if the totals are taken to refer to the whole population, and not to the men of military age alone. Presumably the compilers of P found the two divergent lists, which had been corrupted by three centuries or more of copying, and believed them to go back to the time of Moses. The divergence in the numbers was then easily explained by supposing one list to represent an earlier census than the other.

On the other hand, recent archæological discoveries have warned us against undue skepticism with regard to the age of the material preserved by P. It has quite generally been assumed, for example, that the Priestly Source gives a fanciful account of the Tabernacle, its installation and cult, which at best only reflects priestly ideals of the Exilic Age. Against this attitude the writer wishes to protest most vigorously. A priori, it is quite as unjustifiable as it would be to insist that the description of the Temple of Herod given in the Mishnaic tractate *Middoth* (compiled two centuries after the destruction of the Temple) is a product of the imagination of Tannaitic rabbis. In the latter case we can prove from Josephus that such skepticism is unwarranted. It is true that the interval of more than four centuries between the destruction of the Tabernacle and the Exile suggests that we must be prepared for erroneous reconstruction in detail, but this is a very different thing from wholesale invention, as demanded by orthodox supporters of the school of Wellhausen. Wellhausen himself admitted freely that there was certainly a temple at Shiloh in the time of Eli, and that the original sanctuary of the Ark was probably a tent,[80] but he denied the authenticity of the description of the Tabernacle in Exodus. That this description is highly idealized we may well admit, but that it is deliberately invented in order to carry the priestly conception of Mosaic cult back to his time we deny. Many indications point to a desert background of the Tent of Meeting (*ohel mô'ed,* the term used by P most frequently). Whereas cedar and olive-wood were employed in building the Temple of Solomon, acacia alone is mentioned in the account of the construction of the Tabernacle. The predominant use of goats' hair tent-cloth and of ram-skins and lamb-skins ('ôrôt 'elîm, 'ôrôt teḥashîm, Ex. 25 : 5, etc.) surely rests on authentic tradition. Quite aside from all other considerations, the wholesale deviation from the plans of the Temple of Solomon and of the ideal Temple of Ezekiel remains inexplicable if we must suppose that the Tabernacle is a fanciful construction of Exilic priests. Nor can we explain the admittedly composite structure of the description unless we suppose that it had some tangible background in tradition.

As a result of the tendency to exaggerate the unilateral course of evolution toward cult centralization in Israel, members of the Wellhausen school have consistently tried to reduce the importance of the rôle played by Shiloh and its sanctuary, or even to eliminate it almost entirely. In 1926 and 1928, as mentioned in chapter I, a Danish expedition worked at Shiloh, under the direction of H. Kjaer, with the assistance of Aage Schmidt. The writer stood in particularly close relation to this undertaking from its very beginning, and examined most of the pottery which was unearthed. The results are clear : there was a Middle Bronze occupation, the duration and character of which are uncertain; this was followed, probably after an interval when the site was abandoned, by a very extensive and important occupation in the Early Iron, which lasted from the thirteenth century (possibly from the early twelfth) to the eleventh. On the summit and around the edges of the site no sherds which could certainly be assigned to Early Iron II or to the transition from Early Iron I (tenth–ninth centuries) were discovered during these two campaigns. It would, therefore, seem to be certain that Shiloh was actually destroyed by the Philistines after the battle of Ebenezer and the cap-

ture of the Ark (cir. 1050 B. C.), as is usually supposed by historians (including Wellhausen).[81] Jere-
miah's allusions to the long previous destruction of
Shiloh also receive their explanation. The extent of
the occupation during the EI I was much greater than
at any subsequent age, including the Byzantine. That
writing was known is attested by an inscribed weight,
which has not yet been explained, though the archaic
characters are clear enough. Future campaigns on the
site, carried out with true Danish care, are certain to
yield much additional material regarding the culture
of the period of the Judges, and may eventually discover the site of the temple, which presumably replaced the original *ohel mô'ed,* if our contentions are
correct.

While we cannot go into detail, for lack of space,
with regard to the apparatus of the Mosaic cult, as
described by P, we may refer again to the discussion
of the altar of incense in chapter II, in connection with
our discovery of the top of such an altar in the level
of the tenth or eleventh centuries B. C. at Tell Beit
Mirsim. The description of the altar of incense used
in the Tabernacle (Ex. 30: 1–3) agrees with that of
the *hammânîm* discovered here and in other sites,
though it was considerably larger. Now, the Priestly
Code would never have introduced such a *hammân*
into its Tabernacle unless there had been a warrant
for it in old tradition. During the Prophetic Age the
use of *hammânîm* had been denounced and incense
eliminated from official Mosaic ritual. It is a common view among Biblical scholars to-day that the
seven-branched candlestick of the Tabernacle (Ex.
25: 31 ff., 37: 17 ff.) reflects the Babylonian or even
the Persian period. Unhappily for this a priori con-

ception, however, it is precisely in the Early Iron I—
never afterwards—that we find pottery lamps with
seven places for wicks, the rim of the lamp being
pinched together seven times. Such lamps are found
in Tell Beit Mirsim B, as well as in contemporary
deposits elsewhere in Palestine.[82]

Before leaving the subject of the Tabernacle, we
would like to point out with emphasis that the Wellhausen theory of cult evolution, in its rigid form, is
now being abandoned by the younger generation of
German scholars. Alt and Noth, in brilliant recent
studies, have established the principle of the amphic-
tyonic origin of the twelve tribes of Israel, that is,
they arose as a league of clans, tribes, or towns around
one (sometimes two) central sanctuaries.[83] Whether
the cult center in earliest Israel was at Shechem, as
maintained by Noth, or at Shiloh (followed by
Shechem and Nob-Gibeon), as we maintain, is not
vitally important.[84] Nor need we enter on a discussion of the theory of Noth, that the amphictyony of
twelve tribes was preceded (before the Song of
Deborah) by one of six, or the theory of Haupt and
others (admitted as possible by Alt) that it was
preceded by a Sinaitic amphictyony (the writer's
view).[85] If we admit the necessity of some central
shrine at the beginning of Israelite history, we have
already torn the foundation from under the Wellhausen theory. There is then no further difficulty in
the way of our ninth century date for the bulk of
Deuteronomy (see above), including the nucleus, at
least, of chapter XII. Since, however, the idea of a
central sanctuary faded rapidly with the development
of local particularism, and again after the disruption
of the monarchy, we may still adhere to Wellhausen's

contention, that the movement for a single center of cult became acute in the late seventh century, and that its success is presupposed by the Priestly Code in the sixth.

The entire school of Wellhausen has agreed on a refusal to admit Mosaic monotheism, and a conviction that Israelite monotheism was the result of a gradual process, which did not culminate until the eighth century B. C. It is true that Palestinian archæology cannot contribute directly to the solution of this problem. We should like, however, to call renewed attention to some facts which strongly favour the early appearance of monotheism in Israel. A priori, we should expect that Israelite monotheism would come into existence in an age when monotheistic tendencies were evident in other parts of the ancient world, and not at a time when no such movements can be traced. Now, it is precisely between 1500 and 1200 B. C., *i. e.*, in the Mosaic age, that we find the closest approach to monotheism in the ancient Gentile world before the Persian period.

In Egypt we have the Aton movement, which, as is well known, consisted in the adoration of the solar disk as the visible manifestation of a single deity, whose cult permitted no rivals. In its purest form the Aton heresy represents the culmination of a very ancient development, traceable before the First Dynasty, as Sethe has recently showed.[86] In its ordinary artistic and literary expression it is generally a kind of heliolatry with evident Asiatic elements. Since the parallels between the Aton faith and the Bible have frequently been stressed, we need not enter into a detailed discussion. The differences are fully as great as the resemblances, yet nothing can alter the fact that we have here a close approach to monotheism, a syncretistic religion, which must have appealed to Asiatics living in Egypt, and a system which grew out of the theology of Heliopolis, *i. e.,* of the town which is connected so closely with the traditions of Israel in Egypt. Since the Aton heresy flourished between 1375 and 1350, *i. e.,* about a century before Moses, according to our view of the chronology, the possibility of a connection remains. The writer has stressed the fact that the full name of *YHWH, *Yahweh-asher-yihweh,*[87] which means literally, " He (who) causes to exist what comes into existence," *i. e.,* the Creator of everything that exists, is an exact translation of a rather common Egyptian liturgical formula, applied to the chief god, who is also the creator of the world, according to Egyptian theology.[88] Since the formula in question does not occur elsewhere in the ancient Orient, a certain dependence is unmistakable. Taken in connection with the numerous Egyptian names among the Aaronid priesthood, both at Shiloh and in Jerusalem, some Egyptian influence on Israelite monotheism must be assumed. It may also be observed that none of the formerly accepted occurrences of the name Yahweh in theophorous compounds of the Bronze Age are now admitted by competent scholars. The verbal form which lies at the base of the name occurs in the Amorite name *Yahwî-ilu,* dating from about 2000 B. C.,[89] and probably meaning " It is god who brings into existence." The meaning is identical with that of such Babylonian names as *Mushabshî-Marduk* (Marduk causes to be) and *Mushabshî-ilu* (a god causes to be),[90] as well as with that of Egyptian names formed with the element *s-kh-p-r,*

" to cause to be, bring into existence." The supposed meanings " the one who blows," or " the one who fells," which have been assigned to the Hebrew divine name by some scholars, are quite without a parallel in the whole domain of ancient nomenclature.

If we turn from Egypt to consider the appearance of monotheistic tendencies in Asia we also find the period between 1500 and 1200 indicated. The famous Babylonian text which identifies all important Babylonian deities with some aspect of Marduk—e. g., Zababa is Marduk of battle, Sin is Marduk as illuminer of night, Adad is Marduk of rain—includes two eastern deities, Tishpak and Shuqamuna, a fact which fixes the date of the original in the Cossæan period, i. e., within the time limits just set.[91] Moreover, in the Late Bronze Age, as we know from the tablets of Amarna and Boghaz-köi, as well as from other sources, there was an extraordinarily favourable soil elsewhere in Western Asia for the formation of monotheistic conceptions. Owing to the great mixture of cultures, combined with intimate international relations, syncretism in religion was widespread, and gods with similar functions became identified. Further, certain names were applied to gods worshipped in a great many different places, all of whom were considered by the more sophisticated as variant forms of one and the same great deity. In the treaties between Khatte (land of the Hittites) and Mitanni, from the fourteenth century B. C., we have, for instance, among the gods of the Hittites who are mentioned as witnesses to the oaths of the contracting parties: Teshup of Nirik, Teshup of Khalab (Aleppo), Teshup of Shamukha, etc., etc.; Khepit of Khalpa, Khepit of Uda, Khepit of Kizzuwadna, etc. Among the deities of Mitanni the same treaties mention: Teshup of Kakhat, Teshup of Wasshukanni, Teshup of Irrite.[92] Since each Teshup possessed individual characteristics, the generalized conception of Teshup could hardly restrict itself to the primary function of the god, who brought fertility through the storm which he controlled, but was likely to include so many diverse aspects that Teshup finally became the sole great god—the totality of the manifestations of the separate forms of Teshup. In Syria, for example, the various forms of the storm-god Hadad (equivalent to Teshup) became so generalized that the Syrian storm-god included, as a rule, the attributes of storm-god and sun-god, and received the more inclusive designation "Lord of Heaven," later Ba'al-shamêm (Canaanite) or Ba'al-shamên (Aramaic).[93]

In Canaanite usage this principle received its widest extension. The totality of gods was called elôhîm or elônîm, terms which meant both "gods" and "totality of manifestations of god." The Pharaoh is addressed by his Canaanite vassals in the Amarna letters as "my gods, my sun-god"; "gods" is naturally an inexact translation of the same word which was used by the purely monotheistic Hebrews in the sense of "God." Be'alim was used similarly of the totality of forms of Ba'al, in contrast to the God of Israel. The plural was used in precisely the same way with names of goddesses; 'Ashtaroth means "the totality of manifestations of Astarte," and early became as common as the singular, while the plural of Anath (a sister form of Astarte), Anathoth, was borrowed by the Egyptians in the Eighteenth Dynasty (if not earlier) as the name of that goddess.[94] This tendency was, therefore, active in the Bronze Age, but rapidly stagnated in the Iron Age, in which it remained alive only in stereotyped words and expressions, such as the place-names 'Ashtarôth and 'Anathôth, Hebrew 'ashterôth (haṣ-)ṣôn, meaning literally " the Astartes of the flock," but really " sheep-breeding," and, of course, Hebrew elôhîm, " God." With the renewed emergence of particularism, with concomitant henotheism, in the Early Iron Age, the development of monotheism from polytheism was faced by insuperable obstacles, which were not removed until the Aramæan syncretism of the Persian period. We regard ourselves, therefore, as entirely justified in combining the emergence of monotheism with the Mosaic movement of the thirteenth century B. C., and not with the prophetic movement of the eighth.[95]

In connection with the question of the date of the ethical and social prescriptions of Mosaism, we find a very similar situation. The famous negative confession of the 125th chapter of the Book of the Dead, which duplicates several of the Ten Commandments (aside from being couched in the first person instead of the second person) dates from the New Empire; the oldest manuscripts date from about the fifteenth century B. C. Turning to Mesopotamia we find, again, the same situation. The second tablet of the magical series Shurpu contains a long list of sins and violations of divine tabus which entail subjection to the power of demons. Here again we have some very close parallels to the ethical prescriptions of Mosaism, including several of the Ten Commandments. A. Schott of Bonn has recently pointed out, after a very thorough study of Assyro-Babylonian style, that Shurpu dates from the Cossæan period, i. e., between

1500 and 1200 (1100 at the latest, including the period following the end of the Cossæan Dynasty).[96] While we do not wish to enter into the vexed subject of the origin and date of the Ten Commandments, it may be observed that the very fact that there are several different forms of them which are preserved in the Torah points to a considerable age for their prototype, whatever it may have been.

Our discussion of the present extra-Biblical material bearing on the antiquity of the Mosaic Law at least shows that the tables are now turned. In future, supporters of now antiquated critical views must take the results of ancient Oriental and archæological research into serious consideration, and must yield many of the positions which they have regarded as inexpugnable. The real importance of Wellhausen's work remains; competent scholars can never again defend the priority of the redaction of P, which continues to be the latest Pentateuchal document instead of the earliest. But all of the documents contain much very ancient matter, and the picture of the evolution of Israelite religion drawn by Wellhausen is probably quite as far from the historic truth as that drawn nearly twenty-five hundred years before by the editor of P. We speak of Zoroastrianism and Buddhism, though the amount of dogma and teaching which can certainly be traced back to the founders is very small indeed; we may continue, a fortiori, to speak of Mosaism. The parallels which we have adduced do not in any way diminish the importance of the work of Moses; despite the opportunities provided by the situation which existed in the Late Bronze Age, no other religion even remotely comparable to it appeared, and Mosaism remained absolutely unique.

4. THE AGE OF THE EXILE AND THE RESTORATION

The third of the topics which we have selected for elucidation from archæology is the period of the Exile and the Restoration. Though the latest period of Old Testament history, it is in some respects almost as obscure as the Age of the Patriarchs. This curious fact is due mainly to the confusion which reigns in the work of the Chronicler, our principal source for its history. Several eminent authorities deny that there was a true Exile at all, and are consequently compelled to deny that there was a true Restoration.[97] Other scholars maintain that Ezra followed Nehemiah, instead of preceding him, as assumed by the present recension of the Chronicler's work.[98] The dates of Ezra and Nehemiah, again, vary greatly in the reconstructions proposed by different scholars.[99] It is evident that the historical development of Judaism in this most critical age cannot be properly understood until we can solve the major problems which are involved. Since every possible solution seems to have its protagonists, and since none of them have obtained general recognition in the last thirty years, we must look outside of the Bible, to the results of archæological discovery, for the solution of these enigmas.

The first contribution of importance made by archæology to our knowledge of the post-exilic age came in 1907, with the publication of the most important of the Elephantine papyri, documents written by Egyptian Jews in Aramaic and dated in the fifth century B. C.[100] The complete publication in 1911 [101] made it clear that there was a much more active and heterogeneous Diaspora (Dispersion) in the fifth century than had ever before been supposed.[102] The references to Sanballat, governor of Samaria, and his two sons, as well as to Johanan, high-priest of the Jews in Jerusalem, proved that Nehemiah must be dated in the reign of Artaxerxes I, and not in the reigns of Artaxerxes II or III.[103] They also proved that Sanballat was a Jew by religion, and that he was actually the governor of Samaria, and not some local magnate, as had often been supposed. The famous Passover letter proved that normative Judaism was imposed upon the colonies of the Diaspora by the aid of the Persian Government, in corroboration of the statements in Ezra.[104] The tax-lists of the temple treasury showed that the Judaism of the colony of Elephantine, founded before the close of the Exile, was a very syncretistic religion, with a background which still remains enigmatic.[105] The language of the Elephantine letters shows that the Aramaic of Ezra may easily date back to the fourth century, if not to the end of the fifth, when we bear in mind that all Biblical documents have been repeatedly subjected to modernization and orthographic revision.[106] The language alone undoubtedly forms a powerful argument in favour of the essential authenticity of the Aramaic letters in Ezra, which has been denied by most modern scholars, with the brilliant exception of Eduard Meyer.[107]

The next archæological light on the post-exilic age came partly from Egypt and partly from Transjordan. In 1919 Edgar began to publish the papyri of the Zeno archives, which had been discovered by natives at Gerza in the Faiyum.[108] These papyri not only throw light on all phases of the situation in Palestine during the middle of the third century B. C.; they also enable us to reconstruct in broad outlines the history of the Tobiad dynasty of Ammon.[109] Sprung from a Jewish ancestor, whose home was probably at 'Arâq el-Emîr in southern Gilead, this family furnished a line of governors of Ammon, to which Tobiah the foe of Nehemiah and ally of Sanballat belonged.[110] The tombs of the Tobiad family at 'Arâq el-Emîr have preserved the name of Tobiah, deeply cut into their external wall, and written in an archaic Aramaic script.[111]

After the War, the writer began to study the archæological materials bearing on the age in question, with some clear-cut results, and others which are not clear enough for presentation here. In studying the surface remains of Judæan mounds, he has been more and more impressed by the fact that a large proportion of them exhibit no remains later than EI II, that is, than the Babylonian Exile. There is fortunately a marked difference between the pottery of the pre-exilic and of the post-exilic periods, so that confusion is impossible.[112] Practically all the ancient Judæan sites of the southern Shephelah and the adjacent Negeb, and many in the southern hill-country to the east show no occupation after the Exile (unless in the Roman or Byzantine periods). Illustrations are: Tell el-Khuweilifeh and Tell 'Aiṭûn, as well as Tell Beit Mirsim itself; Tell ed-Duweir (Lachish), Tell ed-Djudeideh, Tell Zakarîyā (Azekah), Khirbet 'Abbâd (Socoh), Khirbet esh-Sheikh Madhkûr (Adullam); Beth-shemesh (in the northern Shephelah); Tell en-Nedjîleh, Tell el-Muleiḥah (southwest of Tell Beit Mirsim); Tell 'Arâd (Arad), Tell Zîf (Ziph), etc., in the southern hill-country to the east. This list does not include numerous smaller sites, nor does it include all the cases where the site was reoccupied after a destruction in the Exilic period, such as Tell eṣ-Ṣâfī, Tell en-Naṣbeh (Ataroth), Tell el-Fûl (Gibeah).[113] In the light of this clear situation, it can no longer be maintained that there was no complete devastation of Judah by the Chaldæans, and no true Exile. If there was an Exile, there must naturally have been a Restoration.

When did the Restoration take place? The Hebrew Ezra (*i. e.,* the standard Hebrew recension of the Chronicler's work) places it under Cyrus, while the Greek recension (Esdras) places it more correctly under Darius I.[114] Archæology has nothing directly to say about the matter, but it has much to say indirectly. By elucidation of the topography and the nomenclature of the list of returned Jews in Ezra 2 and Neh. 7, it proves that Kittel is wrong in considering it as referring to the returned immigrants at the beginning of the reign of Cyrus.[115] Nor can we, as Eduard Meyer and Kittel have proved, explain the list as a much later census of the population of Judæa.[116] The list includes both the returned families (called *benê-N,* or "children of N") and the inhabitants of the villages around Jerusalem who had remained in the land (called *anshê-N,* or "men of N"). These villages are all in the extreme north, and do not include any in the districts which were so thoroughly devastated by the Chaldæans and their allies. There was a later expansion of Jewish territory toward the south, as far as Beth-zur, which thereafter remained the southern boundary of Judæa. This is not the place to discuss the tentative reëstablishment of a Jewish community at the beginning of Cyrus' reign, under Sinabuṣur ("Sheshbazzar"), Zerubbabel's uncle.[117]

The commonly accepted view that Zerubbabel was removed from his post by the Persians during the construction of the Temple has recently been developed most brilliantly by Kittel, who fixes the date of his deposition in 518 B. c.[118] The circumstances surrounding the intended rebellion (there is no evidence of open revolt) of Zerubbabel have now been somewhat clarified by F. W. König's recent discovery that Syria was actually among the Persian provinces which rebelled at the outset of the reign of Darius, and was therefore subdued between 520 (the date of the conquest of Babylonia) and 517 (the date of the subjection of Egypt).[119] Zerubbabel was the last governor of Judæa who belonged to the old royal house; thenceforth the Jewish community became a semi-theocratic state, under Persian political rule, but otherwise under the domination of the high-priest and his advisory council. We have extremely interesting archæological illustrations of this transformation in Jewish polity, as we shall presently see.

In 1926 the writer published a paper [120] in which he discussed three groups of seal-impressions on jar-handles belonging to Early Iron III, found at Jerusalem, Jericho, Gezer, and Tell en-Naṣbeh (Ataroth). It will be noted that all of them come from the direct sphere of the post-exilic Jewish commonwealth, just as all the jar-handles bearing the royal stamp have been found within the bounds of the pre-exilic Judæan state. The three groups may be arranged chronologically by apparently concurrent epigraphical and ceramic indications. First comes a seal-impression

bearing four letters variously distributed on the seal,
but always the same. At first this seal was read
Adaiah (*'Adayah*),[121] but the consideration of Punic
monograms has since imposed the reading Jedaiah
(*Yeda'yah*,[122] the full form of the better known name
Yaddû'). Jedaiah is the name of the most important
priestly family of the post-exilic period, the family to
which the high-priests belonged.[123] The administration
of the temple treasury and the collection of the tithe
from all registered Jews then lay in the hands of the
high-priestly family during the period following the
downfall of Zerubbabel about 518 B. C. The next
oldest group of seal impressions on jar-handles bears
a pentagram, between whose apices are five letters,
forming the name *Shelemyau, i. e.,* Shelemiah. The
meaning of this stamp becomes clear from Neh.
13: 10 ff., where Nehemiah describes his reform of
the corrupt administration of the temple treasury,
which he placed under the superintendence of the
priest Shelemiah.[124] About 432 B. C. the latter superseded the house of Jedaiah, which had controlled the
temple income for nearly ninety years, if we are
correct. No fewer than twenty-one of these stamps
were found on the Ophel hill of Jerusalem by Duncan.
The third and latest of the seals of the temple fiscus
is represented by the stamped jar-handles bearing the
words *Yah* or *Yahu,* which have been found in great
numbers at Jerusalem, Jericho, and Tell en-Naṣbeh.[125]
These stamps are all inscribed in Aramaic instead of
Hebrew characters, and must cover a long period, to
judge from the variation in the forms of the letters.
We may date them provisionally between 400 and
300 B. C., and suppose that they extend down to the
beginning of the Ptolemaic period.

While it would be hazardous to draw far-reaching historical conclusions from the sequence of these three groups of stamped jar-handles, a few deductions are in order. In the first place, it is interesting to note that the two Hebrew groups present transitional forms of the characters, reminding us of seventh and sixth century script on the one hand and of somewhat later Aramaic forms on the other. Hebrew gives way to Aramaic about 400 B. C., just when one would expect, since Nehemiah and Malachi are the last books of the Bible to be written in good classical Hebrew, and both date from the second half of the fifth century. The work of the Chronicler already shows a strong Aramaic influence; the use of Hebrew for literary purposes was being abandoned in his time. Later Hebrew books, where not merely editions of older works, show an increasingly artificial style, with more and more Aramaic elements. Another interesting fact is that about 400 B. C. we find the use of family and personal names given up, and replaced by the name of God in the abbreviated forms *Yahu* and *Yah*. This can hardly be separated from the increasingly theocratic character of the Jewish community in Judæa. Nehemiah was the last layman to interfere effectively with the priestly constitution, by virtue of the powers invested in him by the Persian crown. Then came the work of the priest Ezra, also with royal authorization, in organizing the theocracy, with the high-priest at the head, in the form which it maintained until the time of the Seleucids.

In concluding our brief sketch of the light shed by archæology on certain Biblical problems, we wish to emphasize again that it does not support either the extreme radical school of Biblical scholars or the ultra-conservative wing. On the whole, the work of moderate critics, such as S. R. Driver, one of the few great Biblical scholars of modern times, is not so greatly affected by it. Driver, with his clear insight into the nature of philological and historical method, seldom expressed himself positively except where the evidence justified it. His views with regard to the date of books and documents seem rarely to be proved absolutely wrong. Even he, however, came, for lack of evidence, to natural, but wholly false results concerning the nature of the patriarchal stories of Genesis. Together with all the other members and friends of the Wellhausen school, he also adopted false premises for his analysis of the historical evolution of Mosaic religion, and arrived very logically at erroneous results. It was, accordingly, the acceptance of untrue philosophical and historical premises that misled Biblical scholars, since no amount of logical reasoning and sound method can compensate for the lack of a solid foundation. Conservative scholars are, we believe, entirely justified in their vigorous denunciation of all efforts to prove the existence of fraudulent invention and deliberate forgery in the Bible. They are equally within their rights in objecting most emphatically to the introduction of a spurious mythology and a thinly veiled paganism into the Bible. We must remember that myths and folklore were early made vehicles of instruction by the use of the allegorical method, both in Egypt and in Mesopotamia, and that we have ample reason to interpret such stories as the Fall allegorically; we must consider the nature of poetic imagery and the transmission of oral history, as described above, and must bear in mind that these are all processes characteristic of the human mind. Many ancient ideas regarding the Bible, and many more modern views concerning it must be abandoned, but the progress of archæological investigation will make the Bible stand out more and more brightly against the background of the ancient Orient.

APPENDIX

[1] For the launching of the Oriental Institute and its original programme see Breasted, *Oriental Institute Communications* No. 1 (=AJSL 38, 233–328) ; for its subsequent development see especially the *General Circulars.* The most important publications for our purpose appear in two series: *Oriental Institute Communications,* a series of preliminary reports, in popular form; *Oriental Institute Publications,* which include definitive publications. There is now a steady stream of publications, all characterized by the highest standards of method and precision.

[2] For the work of the Schools see the *Bulletin,* a quarterly describing in concise and popular fashion what the Schools are doing in the archæological field; it is edited by the writer. More elaborate preliminary reports, as well as some definitive publications, appear in the *Annual* (Vol. I, 1920). Other series of publications have been launched, but do not, so far, touch our field so closely. For information one should write to Professor J. A. Montgomery, University of Pennsylvania, Philadelphia (president of the Schools), or to Professor Mary I. Hussey, Mount Holyoke College, South Hadley, Mass. (A dollar sent to Miss Hussey will secure a year's subscription to the *Bulletin.*) The present director of the School in Jerusalem is Professor Millar Burrows.

[3] See Robinson, *Biblical Researches in Palestine, Mount Sinai and Arabia Petræa,* 3 vols., London, 1841, with the supplementary volume embodying his later explorations and researches, *Later Biblical Researches in*

Palestine and the Adjacent Regions, London, 1856. For an account of his life see *Life, Writings, and Character of Edward Robinson,* New York, 1863.

[4] It is quite true that great progress has been made since Robinson's day in the study of topography. A still more critical study of tradition (recognizing its inherent importance), a great advance in the field of comparative linguistics (with a vastly better comprehension of the limits, as well as of the possibilities, of the comparison of ancient and modern place-names), and above all the unprecedented development of our knowledge of archæology (especially the use of pottery in order to date ancient sites) have led to very much more precise results. The principal work in this field since the War has been done by Professor Albrecht Alt of the University of Leipzig and by the writer. Our pupils are now carrying this work on with very good results; one may single out for special notice in this connection the admirable work of a young Finnish scholar, Dr. Aapeli Saarisalo.

[5] For Robertson Smith's views see the ninth edition of the *Encyclopædia Britannica,* s. v. *Jerusalem,* while the views of Conder are expressed in Hastings' *Dictionary of the Bible,* the *Encyclopædia Biblica,* etc., and Wilson's may be found conveniently in the second edition of Smith's *Dictionary of the Bible.*

[6] Driver, *Modern Research as Illustrating the Bible,* London, 1909. This book may still be read with great profit. Driver's topographical articles are mostly better than those of Wilson and Conder.

[7] The only archæological explorer of this generation who merits special attention is Guérin, whose travels and publications were both more extensive and more elaborate than those of Robinson, but whose critical method was incomparably inferior, and who, consequently, made very few identifications which have stood the test of time; see his *Description de la Palestine* in eight volumes, Paris, 1868–1889.

[8] For a full and delightfully written account of his detection and exposure of the Shapira forgeries, including both the Moabite antiquities and the archetype of Deuteronomy, see Clermont-Ganneau, *Les fraudes archéologiques en Palestine,* Paris, 1885. The standpoint of the Shapira family has been vividly described by the daughter of the forger, Mme. Harry, in her charming autobiographical romance, *La petite fille de Jérusalem,* translated into English as *The Little Daughter of Jerusalem.* Clermont-Ganneau appears here as Merle-Vanneau.

[9] Later Lord Kitchener of Khartum, commander-in-chief of the British army in the World War.

[10] For the organization and history of the Palestine Exploration Fund see especially the *Quarterly Statement* of the Fund, which has appeared continuously since the year 1869. In recent years the quarterly has been supplemented by a somewhat irregularly appearing *Annual.* The numerous other publications of the Fund are listed in every *Quarterly Statement.*

[11] See *The Survey of Western Palestine,* three vols., London, 1881–3 (with a number of supplementary volumes of name-lists, geology, etc.) ; *Jerusalem,* 1884; *Survey of Eastern Palestine,* 1889 (only one volume appeared, since the work of the survey was broken off before completion). The map of Western Palestine appeared in twenty-six sheets, on the scale of an inch to the mile.

[12] For full bibliography of the literature on this subject see Schürer, *Geschichte des jüdischen Volkes im Zeitalter Jesu Christi,* Vol. III, 4th ed., (Leipzig, 1909), pp. 170–72.

[13] Cf. Wilson and Warren, *The Recovery of Jerusalem,* London, 1871.

[14] Some of the most important tells of Palestine were omitted from the maps of the Survey for the same reason.

¹⁵ See ZDPV 4–5 (1881–2).

¹⁶ See Petrie, *Tell el Hesy,* London, 1891, as well as the reports in the *Quarterly Statement* for 1890 and 1891.

¹⁷ See Bliss, *A Mound of Many Cities,* London, 1894.

¹⁸ Conder, QS 1891, 69 and elsewhere; Nowack, *Lehrbuch der hebräischen Archäologie,* Vol. I, p. 265 (1894).

¹⁹ Bliss and Macalister, *Excavations in Palestine during 1898–1900,* London, 1902.

²⁰ Cf. *Proceedings of the American Philosophical Society,* Vol. 69, p. 442 f.

²¹ See Macalister, *The Excavation of Gezer,* 3 vols., London, 1912.

²² Cf. Vincent, RB 1923, 552 ff.; 1924, 161 ff.

²³ The *mêm* in this tablet is archaic, while the *kaf* is already formed like the classical Hebrew type. A date in the second half of the tenth century is probable.

²⁴ Sellin, *Tell Ta'annek,* Vienna, 1904 (*Denkschriften d. Kais. Akad. d. Wiss., Phil.-hist. Klasse,* Vol. 50, part 4); *Eine Nachlese auf dem Tell Ta'annek,* Vienna, 1906 (*Denkschriften,* Vol. 52, part 3).

²⁵ For this reading of the name see JPOS 4, 140, n. 3, and Gustavs, ZDPV 1928, 196 f. (=*Die Personennamen in den Tontafeln von Tell Ta'annek,* p. 45 f.).

²⁶ JPOS 2, 132, on which see Gustavs, *op. cit.,* p. 57 f. The reason for my failure to publish my promised article on these tablets is that when I was in Constantinople for the purpose of collating them, there happened to be no responsible museum official there to give me the requisite permission.

²⁷ See especially Gustavs, *op. cit.*

²⁸ Schumacher and Steuernagel, *Tell el-Mutesellim,* Vol. I, Leipzig, 1908; Watzinger, Vol. II, 1929.

²⁹ See Kautzsch, *Mitteilungen und Nachrichten des Deutschen Palästina-Vereins,* 1904, p. 2.

³⁰ Sellin and Watzinger, *Jericho,* Leipzig, 1913.

³¹ On the chronology of Jericho see Vincent, RB 1930,

403 ff., with full reference to the discussions by Albright and Watzinger. The writer proposes to discuss the subject elsewhere, after the publication of Garstang's results. The first campaign of the latter, in 1930, produced further confirmation of the high chronology, against the low, which is maintained by Vincent. Garstang himself believes that Jericho fell about 1400 B. C. —a date which appears rather too low to the writer.

[32] Reisner, Fisher, and Lyon, *The Harvard Excavations at Samaria,* 2 vols., Cambridge, 1924.

[33] It is the merit of Professor D. G. Lyon to have projected the excavation and to have interested Mr. Schiff in it.

[34] Usually identified with Jeroboam II. An identification with another monarch of the house of Jehu is also possible.

[35] See Albright, JPOS 5, 28–31, 38–43; Dussaud, *Samarie au temps d'Achab* (=*Syria,* Vols. 6–7, especially 7, p. 9 ff.) ; Noth, ZDPV 50, 219–40.

[36] The dialect of the Mesha stone used to be considered as a sort of border speech, showing a mixture of Hebrew, Aramaic, and Arabic elements. The discovery of the ostraca of Samaria, as well as of the Amarna tablets and of the archaic Phœnician inscriptions of Byblos have showed that it is a purely Canaanite (Hebrew) dialect, and that it is virtually identical (so far as our material permits us to say) with the language of the Northern Kingdom and of Phœnicia. The only certain divergence is in the plural ending, which was *nûn* instead of *mêm* in Moabite, just as in Amorite, whereas in the other Canaanite dialects we find *mêm.*

[37] This date (formerly given as 722) is now established by Begrich. However, it remains, of course, in the Assyrian calendar year 722/1, so the modification is very slight indeed.

[38] See below, p. 170.

[39] Work was recommenced at Samaria in the spring of

1931, under the joint auspices of Harvard University, the Palestine Exploration Fund, and the Hebrew University, and under the direction of Mr. J. W. Crowfoot.

⁴⁰ See Vincent, *Jérusalem sous terre*, London, 1911.

⁴¹ But not so far back as is often assumed; see *Jewish Quarterly Review*, 1930, p. 165 f., and Gjerstad, *Studies on Prehistoric Cyprus*, p. 302 f.

⁴² The excavations carried on at Beth-shemesh by Mackenzie and at Shechem by Sellin will be described below; for the work accomplished by Weill at the southern end of the Davidic Jerusalem (Ophel) see his book *La cité de David*, Paris, 1920.

⁴³ For the work of the École Biblique see the principal publication, *Revue Biblique*, now in its fortieth year. This journal contains more important archæological information than any other periodical dealing with the Bible or with Palestine.

⁴⁴ The *Journal of the Palestine Oriental Society*, which has appeared continuously since 1921, is a strictly international publication, with articles in various languages. It is edited by Canon H. Danby, D.D., St. George's Close, Jerusalem, to whom subscriptions may be sent ($5.00 a year).

⁴⁵ The publications of the Hebrew University in the field of Palestine archæology are becoming more and more important, owing to the activity of E. L. Sukenik, Field Archæologist of the University.

⁴⁶ See the *Palästinajahrbuch*, which gives annual accounts of the valuable work carried on before the War by Dalman, and since by Alt.

⁴⁷ The British School is now combined with the Palestine Exploration Fund in a joint organization. Its director, Mr. J. W. Crowfoot, is now in charge of the work of the Fund in Palestine, and the news of the School appears in the *Quarterly Statement* instead of in a separate organ, the *Bulletin of the British School of Archæology*, as was the case under Garstang's direction, for

the first years after the War. Close relations have always subsisted between the British and the American Schools in Jerusalem; the former housed our library for a number of years, and our institution now houses the library of the British School.

[48] For the work of this school, under the direction of Père A. Mallon, see *Biblica,* the organ of the Pontifical Biblical Institute at Rome.

[49] *Deutsche Literaturzeitung,* 1926, col. 1913 f.

[50] See Rowe, *The Topography and History of Beth-shan,* Philadelphia, 1930; Fitzgerald, *The Pottery,* 1930; numerous articles by Fisher and Rowe in the *Museum Journal* since 1922.

[51] For the god Makal see Vincent, RB 1928, 512 ff.; Rowe, *Beth-shan,* p. 14 f. On the closely related god Resheph see Albright, *Haupt Anniversary Volume,* p. 143 ff. The writer has a paper on these deities in preparation.

[52] See Rowe, *Beth-shan,* p. 15 f. and frontispiece.

[53] See Rowe, *Beth-shan,* p. 11 f., with references to his more extended descriptions elsewhere.

[54] Cf. I Sam. 1:24–5, referred to by Rowe.

[55] Rowe, *Beth-shan,* p. 41 f., and Fitzgerald, *Pottery,* p. 17, are mistaken in supposing that the acropolis was occupied during the period from 1000 B. C. to the Greek period. Whereas quantities of pottery belonging to Early Iron I have been found (only a selection of the pottery of this period found in two campaigns is given by Fitzgerald), nothing from Early Iron II and III (tenth to fourth centuries) has so far been discovered. The vases mentioned by Fitzgerald are quite certainly from Early Iron I.

[56] Rowe, *Beth-shan,* p. 33 ff.

[57] Rowe, *Beth-shan,* p. 29; see below, p. 206, n. 8.

[58] Cf. ZAW 1929, 9, n. 3.

[59] See the preliminary reports by Fisher, *Or. Inst. Comm.,* No. 4, 1929, and by Guy, No. 9, 1931.

[60] The contrast between the masonry of Solomon's time found at Megiddo and Gezer, and that of Saul's time, found by the writer at Tell el-Fûl (see below), is very great, and illustrates the corresponding transformation of Israelite culture very well indeed.

[61] See *Archiv für Orientforschung*, Vol. 6, p. 219 f.

[62] See the writer's *Excavations at Gibeah of Benjamin*, 1924 (*Annual*, Vol. 4).

[63] See *Bulletin*, No. 14, p. 2 ff.; *Annual*, Vol. 6, p. 56 ff.; Mallon, *Biblica*, Vol. 5, p. 413 ff.; Kyle, *Explorations in Sodom*, New York, 1928. The complete account of the results of our expedition has not yet been published.

[64] The writer hopes to publish an account of this important site, with plans and photographs, in the near future.

[65] Power's attempt to locate Sodom and Gomorrah at the northern end of the Dead Sea is quite unconvincing; see Abel, RB 1931, pp. 380–400.

[66] See below, p. 134.

[67] See below, *loc. cit.*

[68] On this question see Hertzberg, ZAW 1929, 161 ff. Hertzberg and I have since reached the definite conclusion that Tell en-Naṣbeh represents Ataroth Archi (cf. *Bulletin*, No. 35, 4). The question will be discussed fully in another place.

[69] See Badè, *Excavations at Tell en-Naṣbeh* 1926 and 1927, Berkeley, 1928; QS 1930, p. 8 ff.

[70] Cf. *Annual*, Vol. 4, p. 92.

[71] See Grant, *Beth Shemesh*, Haverford, 1929; *Annual*, Vol. 9, p. 1 ff.

[72] See *Annuals* I and II of the Palestine Exploration Fund (1911–13).

[73] Some earlier pottery has been found, carrying us back to the transition from Early to Middle Bronze (not before about 2000 B. C.), but the oldest stratified remains so far found do not antedate the latter part of the

Middle Bronze. Mackenzie supposed that the town was destroyed by Sennacherib, but since then a number of stamped jar-handles of the latest pre-exilic type (seventh century B. C.) have been found, both by Grant and by members of the American School in walking over the mound, so that we must date its destruction at the time of the last Chaldæan invasion.

[74] See RB 1930, 401 f. The writer is absolutely convinced of the early date (not later than the fourteenth century B. C.), because of the circumstances of discovery alone. Dussaud and others are mistaken in lowering its date by several centuries. The archaic *mêm* (which is absolutely certain) alone forces us to go back before 900 B. C., while the prostrate *het* forms a connecting link with the Sinai alphabet. The form of the *aleph* here found is in reality older than that of the Akhîrâm inscription, while there are a number of curious letters, which cannot yet be identified.

[75] See the excavators' reports in QS 1921–2.

[76] Among them we may mention soundings at Harbadj, Tell 'Amr and Tell el-Qassîs in Galilee, all under Garstang's direction, soundings in Gaza, and excavations by Garstang at Dor (Ṭanṭûrah). On the results see especially *Bulletin of the British School of Archæology*, Nos. 2 and 4.

[77] See *Annual* IV and V of the Palestine Exploration Fund, by Macalister, Duncan, Crowfoot, and Fitzgerald (cf. the writer's review, *Jewish Quarterly Review*, 1930, pp. 163–8).

[78] For Weill's work before the War see *La cité de David*, Paris, 1920; his work since the War, which led to singularly few interesting discoveries, has not yet been published.

[79] Against the view that this revetment is " Jebusite " see *Jewish Quarterly Review*, 1930, p. 167 f.

[80] See now Alt, *Das Taltor von Jerusalem* (*Palästina-*

jahrbuch, 1928, p. 74 ff.), and the writer's observation, *loc. cit.*

[81] See Flinders Petrie, *Gerar,* London, 1928. The chronology of this publication is not reliable, since the distinguished author follows the practice of working out his chronology without reference to the results of any other scholar; cf. ZAW 1929, 9, n. 2, and Galling, ZAW 1929, 242–50.

[82] See Petrie, *Beth-Pelet* I, London, 1930, and preliminary reports in *Ancient Egypt* since 1928. The chronology of this site is relatively satisfactory back to the end of the Middle Bronze. The valuable correlation between Egyptian and Palestinian scarab chronology which he establishes leads to the most fanciful results in absolute dating, since Petrie still adheres to his theory of an abnormally high duration of the Hyksos sway in Egypt—a conception which flagrantly contradicts the evidence from other sites of Palestine.

[83] The only consonants of the two names which correspond are the first; Hebrew *p* becomes *f* in Arabic. The others are entirely distinct, and the vocalization of the two names is absolutely different. Vowels are just as important as consonants, though subject, of course, to other laws.

[84] The identification often suggested of Sharuhen with Tell esh-Sheriʻah northeast of Tell el-Fârʻah is quite impossible. In favour of our identification is the fact that Sharuhen was an important Hyksos center, and was occupied in the time of Shishak, facts which are both equally true of Tell el-Fârʻah.

[85] See JSOR 10, 245–54; Petrie, *Ancient Egypt,* 1929, p. 1 ff.; Albright, *Archiv für Orientforschung,* Vol. 6, p. 219, n. 8.

[86] See the account of the first campaign in QS 1930, 123 ff.

[87] See Sellin's preliminary reports in the *Anzeiger* of the Vienna Academy of Sciences, 1914, and in ZDPV

1926–8; see also Böhl, *De geschiedenis der stad Sichem en de opgravingen aldaar,* Amsterdam, 1926 (*Mededeelingen d. Kon. Ak. w. Wet., afd. Let.,* 62B, No. 1).

[88] See Böhl, ZDPV 49 (1926), 321 ff.

[89] See especially H. Kjaer, *The Excavation of Shiloh,* Jerusalem, 1930 (=JPOS 1930, 87–174).

[90] Cf. below, p. 159 f.

[91] See Kohl and Watzinger, *Antike Synagogen in Galilæa,* Leipzig, 1916.

[92] See Orfali, *Capharnaum et ses ruines,* Paris, 1922. Père Orfali was killed in an automobile accident, April, 1926, while returning from his beloved Capernaum to attend the opening session of the international congress of archæologists. He was the first Oriental to distinguish himself as a Palestinian archæologist.

[93] This view is shared by the three leading authorities, Watzinger, Vincent, and Sukenik. The latter is preparing an elaborate work on the synagogues, which will greatly advance our knowledge of them.

[94] RB 1921, 442 ff., 579 ff. The definitive publication has not yet appeared, though ready for press.

[95] Sukenik's publication of the Beth Alpha synagogue is in press. Cf. provisionally the account by McCown in the *Bulletin,* No. 37, p. 16 f. (cuts on pp. 13–19).

[96] Cf. McCown, *Bulletin,* No. 37, p. 15 f.

[97] Sukenik has also made some very important discoveries of inscribed ossuaries (bone-boxes) from the last century of the Second Temple (cir. 30 B. C.–70 A. D.) in the vicinity of Jerusalem; a monograph on the ossuaries is in preparation. In collaboration with L. A. Mayer he has also traced the line of the third wall of Jerusalem, begun by Herod Agrippa and completed by the Jewish rebels between 66 and 70 A. D.; see their book, *The Third Wall of Jerusalem,* Jerusalem, 1930.

[98] The expedition of the Duc de Luynes in 1864 was the first to call attention to the existence of flint artifacts in Syria and Palestine, and the Abbé Moretain then

began his collection of artifacts from the environs of Bethlehem.   See the historical sketch given by Karge, *Rephaim,* Paderborn, 1917, p. 10 ff.

[99] See Zumoffen, *La Phénicie avant les Phéniciens,* Beyrouth, 1900.

[100] Karge, *op. cit.*

[101] See Turville-Petre, *Researches in Prehistoric Galilee,* London, 1927.

[102] See her preliminary reports in QS since 1928.

[103] Neuville has also made important discoveries in other fields of prehistory; cf. JPOS 10, 64 ff., 193 ff.

[104] See *Biblica,* 1930, p. 3 ff.   [In the 1930–31 campaign Mallon discovered an astonishing collection of sherds bearing linear characters, often in groups, and of pebbles with elaborate symbolic carvings, all from the chalcolithic of the third millennium B. C.; see *Biblica,* 1931, 257 ff.]

[105] Cf. already *Annual,* Vol. 6, p. 66 ff.

[106] For accurate and comprehensive surveys of the field of Palestinian archæology, nothing in any language can rival the work of P. Thomsen; see especially his two compact handbooks, *Kompendium der palästinischen Altertumskunde* (Tübingen, 1913), and his *Palästina und seine Kultur* (Leipzig, 1931).   In his *Palästina-Literatur* (4 vols., Leipzig, 1911–1927), the student will find an exhaustive bibliography of recent literature.

NOTES ON CHAPTER II

[1] *Bulletin*, No. 15, p. 4 f.

[2] The first two campaigns were conducted as joint expeditions of Xenia Theological Seminary and the American School in Jerusalem, while the third campaign, following the union of Xenia with the Pittsburgh Theological Seminary of the United Presbyterian Church, was a joint excavation of the Pittsburgh-Xenia Theological Seminary and the American School. Dr. Kyle acted throughout as president of the staff of the expedition, while the writer directed the work.

[3] For the results of the first campaign see provisionally *Bulletin*, No. 23, pp. 2–14; Kyle, *Bibliotheca Sacra*, 1926, pp. 378–402; and Kyle's letters to the *Sunday School Times* during the summer of 1926.

[4] See *Bulletin*, No. 31, pp. 1–11; ZAW 1929, pp. 1–17; Kyle, *Bibliotheca Sacra*, 1928, pp. 381–408; Kyle's letters to the *Sunday School Times* during the summer of 1928.

[5] See *Bulletin*, No. 39, pp. 1–10; a paper in JPOS, 1931; Kyle, *Bibliotheca Sacra*, 1930, pp. 382–404; letters to the *Sunday School Times,* as before.

[6] Besides the two heads of the expedition, there were Professor J. L. Kelso of Xenia and two students of the same institution, the Revs. Lee and Webster.

[7] The practicality and manual skill of young Americans is of the greatest utility in an excavation. In the long run, however, interest tends to flag unless supported by a sound training, either in architecture and museum craft, or in philological and historical science. This is one reason why so few Americans continue in archæological work.

[8] The surveyor, William Gad, and the foremen, men with years of excavating experience, were of great as-

sistance to us, especially since the writer's health was rather poor.

[9] The foreign members of the staff, besides the heads, were Dr. Aage Schmidt, Professor Robert Montgomery of Pittsburgh (now president of Tarkio College, Mo.), and Dr. Paul Culley, a graduate of Johns Hopkins Medical School. Dr. Schmidt's devoted assistance was of the greatest value, and some of our best results are due to him. Dr. Culley ran an informal clinic for the Arabs of the neighbourhood, and helped to create a friendly atmosphere—besides, of course, assisting with the archæological work.

[10] Besides the heads there were Professor O. R. Sellers of the Presbyterian Theological Seminary in Chicago, Professor J. L. Kelso of the Pittsburgh-Xenia Seminary, Dr. Aage Schmidt, Dr. Nelson Glueck of Hebrew Union College, and Dr. A. Saarisalo of the University of Helsinki. All seven foreign members of the staff paid their own travelling expenses from their respective homes to Palestine and back—a record which it would be hard to beat, since all of them are men of extremely modest means.

[11] Labib Sorial, William Gad, and Bulos el-A'radj, the first two of whom are Egyptians, and the third a Palestinian. Labib took charge of the contour work and William of the detail planning.

[12] The family name is *Abū 'Arqûb,* a *kunyah* derived from a word meaning " tendon of Achilles," but is itself of obscure origin. The collective is *'Arâqbeh,* and the current form is a double collective.

[13] The Gerza papyri have thrown new light on the history and name of Adora; see Abel, RB 1924, 566.

[14] Cf. Robinson, *Biblical Researches in Palestine,* Vol. III, p. 3 f.

[15] See Haddad, JPOS I, 209 ff.

[16] This name is not a collective, but is the *kunyah* of the founder of the clan, literally " Father of Drachmas."

The same *kunyah* was common in the Middle Ages, and was borne by several eminent Arab scholars.

[17] There is some doubt about the tribal affiliation, and I have heard other views expressed.

[18] Cf. Gen. 34; 12 ff.; the narratives of the Conquest in Joshua and Judges.

[19] The writer plans to publish this material elsewhere.

[20] The weight is 4.565 kilograms.

[21] Cf. ZAW 1929, 2 and note 2.

[22] For the exact definition and delimitation of these terms see G. A. Smith, *Historical Geography of the Holy Land*.

[23] The name is probably derived from the name of the Mamluk sultan al-Malik az-Zâhir Baibars (1260–77 A. D.) or al-Malik az-Zâhir Barqûq (1382–98), the first of whom made a profound impression on Palestine by his activity in building and administration, as illustrated by numerous places called ez-Zâherîyeh.

[24] The name is purely Arabic and throws no light on the identification.

[25] The Arabic name means " Mother of Pomegranates " (*Rummân*=Heb. *rimmôn*).

[26] The name *'Aiṭûn* is unquestionably of Hebrew origin, and may represent an Etam, despite the different ending. However, the identification sometimes given with the Etam of Simeon is topographically impossible.

[27] Cf. ZAW 1929, 3.

[28] *Barsamâ* and *Barsimiâ* are both common Aramaic names; for the change of *b* to *m* by dissimilation cf. *Ma'albekk* for *Ba'albekk* (Baalbek) and *Khirbet Mekîkā* for *Khirbet Beit Kîkā* (a ruin northwest of Jerusalem), the latter parallel being particularly close (*Beit *Birsim > Beit Mirsim*).

[29] For the name, its original form (Kiriath-sopher), and parallels from the Bronze Age see ZAW 1929, 2, note 3.

[30] Cf. *Proceedings of the American Philosophical Society,* Vol. 69 (1930), p. 448 f.

[31] See Jos. 10:38 f.; 15:13 ff.; Jud. 1:10 ff.; 3:9 ff. The ascription of this achievement to Joshua in one passage illustrates the general tendency to simplify the complicated story of the Conquest, and to connect all its phases with the great Israelite hero Joshua.

[32] Klein has supposed that the statement of the seventh century (A. D.) liturgical poet Kalir that his home was in Kiriath-sepher is to be taken literally, but other Jewish scholars consider it as metaphorical, referring to the " Book-city," *i. e.,* probably Tiberias.

[33] The identification of Gerar with Tell Djemmeh is almost entirely based on similar topographical and archæological evidence; the onomastic argument from the name of the neighbouring Byzantine village ruin now called Khirbet Umm ed-Djerâr, *i. e.,* " Mother of Jars," is not convincing. I have no doubt whatever that the identification is correct.

[34] Against this combination see, *e. g.,* ZAW 1929, 3, note 2.

[35] Against this identification see *Annual,* Vols. II/III, pp. 1–17.

[36] See above, p. 187, note 83. It should be added that the Arabic name is not only wholly different from the Hebrew, but has a perfectly good Arabic meaning, " Mound of the Eminence (Ridge)."

[37] See above, p. 185, note 68.

[38] Even to-day the timber returns if it is given half a chance. The conifers have, however, been almost extirpated, and require some cultivation to give them a renewed start. After a grove of conifers has once been started, there is no further difficulty; it grows and extends without human aid.

[39] For the time and nature of the Amorite occupation see JPOS 8, 250 ff.

[40] See above, p. 48, and below, p. 134.

[41] See below, p. 136.

[42] See Bliss, *A Mound of Many Cities,* pp. 18–43. For the same period elsewhere in Palestine cf. the full discussion of EB pottery by Karge, *Rephaim,* pp. 223–293. Most previous accounts confuse EB pottery with MB, and often fail to distinguish Neolithic from MB.

[43] For this type of pottery see Sellin and Watzinger, *Jericho,* p. 108 ff. Essentially the same kind of incised decoration appears contemporaneously in Egypt; *e. g.,* Brunton, *Qau and Badari III* (1930), plates XII–XVIII.

[44] See for the fullest account of this pottery Junker, *Der nubische Ursprung der sogenannten Tell el-Jahūdīye-Vasen (Akad. d. Wiss. in Wien, Phil.-hist. Kl., Sitzb.,* 198, 3, 1921). Junker's thesis is, however, quite certainly wrong; the Syrian origin of this pottery is established (cf. Bonnet, *Zeitschrift für Ægyptische Sprache,* Vol. 59, p. 119 ff.).

[45] Cf. *Bulletin,* No. 29, p. 4 ff.; No. 35, pp. 3, 10; Karge, *Rephaim,* pp. 352–79. Karge had a tendency to antedate these remains, which probably are not older than the end of the third millennium, and may in part descend to the middle of the second.

[46] *Gezer,* Vol. I, pp. 111–141; III, plates xxxii–xlii; for an elaborate archæological discussion see Vincent, RB 1924, 161–185. The latter gave the limits 1800–1600 for these tombs, and the predominance of elaborate curvilinear design on the scarabs, together with the diversity of graceful shapes in pottery, seems to point clearly to the Thirteenth Dynasty, *i. e.,* the eighteenth century B. C. Our G pottery naturally contains a very high proportion of crude pottery, since it comes from a house, not from a tomb.

[47] See the description, with photograph, *Bulletin,* No. 31, pp. 3, 6.

[48] See below, p. 95 f.

[49] Grant, *Annual,* Vol. 9, p. 2; *Beth Shemesh,* p. 35.

[50] The Mexican earth-goddess is represented with a

serpent crawling into her vulva; for similar representations in India see Penzer, *The Ocean of Story,* Vol. II, p. 307, n. 2; cf. also AJSL 36, 272, above.

[51] See the illustrations AOTB II, Nos. 271, 276.

[52] See the discussion of serpent-goddesses AJSL 36, 271 ff.

[53] See Evans, *Palace of Minos,* passim.

[54] See *Bulletin,* No. 39, pp. 6, 9 (illustration). The set will be discussed fully by the writer in the first volume of *Mizraim.*

[55] The game is almost certainly of Egyptian origin, and did not come from the east, as supposed by Ranke, *Ægypten und ægyptisches Leben im Altertum,* 2nd ed., p. 291.

[56] The skeletal material was carefully examined and identified by Dr. Paul Culley, who was a member of our staff during the second campaign.

[57] Two exactly similar scarabs, with the same inscription, are published by Hall, *Catalogue of Egyptian Scarabs,* Nos. 1811–2 (p. 181).

[58] For similar scarabs see Hall, *op. cit.,* Nos. 2214–5, 2217 (pp. 221–2), which not only agree in showing the king smiting an Asiatic prisoner with the Egyptian *khepesh* sword, but also in placing the *weser* sign behind the Pharaoh; cf. also Petrie, *Scarabs and Cylinders,* plate XL, Nos. 24–5.

[59] See *Bulletin,* No. 39, pp. 5, 7 (with illustrations).

[60] See AOTB II, No. 399.

[61] For the position flanking the pedestal or throne cf. the throne of Solomon, the representation of Atargatis on a pedestal flanked by two lions (AOTB II, No. 277), etc., etc.

[62] Illustrations of the lion-deity standing on a lion or seated on a throne supported by two lions are extremely numerous; one may refer to various representations of Atargatis, to Qadesh on the lion, to Hadad of Sham'al standing on a pedestal supported by two lions, to the

unidentified Syrian god (Ba'al-hammân?) shown standing on a lion in a stele from the Persian period found in Egypt (AOTB II, No. 354), to the god of Marathus (AOTB II, No. 307), etc., etc.

[63] See Vincent, RB 1928, 540 ff.

[64] For Resheph see *Haupt Anniversary Volume,* p. 143 ff., and Cook, *The Religion of Ancient Palestine in the Light of Archæology,* London, 1930, p. 112 ff. The writer hopes to discuss the gods Rashap (Resheph), Makal, and Ginai elsewhere in the near future.

[65] The view that she was primarily a chthonic deity is quite compatible with the undoubted fact that she was identified at a very early date with Astarte, the Queen of Heaven. The writer expects to resume his study of 'Anat elsewhere.

[66] See, *e. g.,* AOTB II, Nos. 287, 291.

[67] AOTB II, Nos. 270, 272; Cook, *Religion of Ancient Palestine,* plate XXIV, Nos. 2–3.

[68] The masculine form *Qadesh,* " sacred," shows perhaps that the name is to be treated as a noun (cf. the equally masculine form *'Ashtar, Ishtar*) rather than as an adjective. In Biblical Hebrew the masculine form means " gallus," while the feminine *qedeshah* (Assyr. *qadishtu*) means " female courtesan." It is also possible that the masculine was used for both male and female prostitutes in other Canaanite dialects.

[69] Cf. AJSL 41, 83: the Syrian goddesses 'Anat and 'Ashtart are called in an Egyptian text, " the great goddesses who conceive but do not bear."

[70] See ZAW 1929, 8.

[71] The writer expects to discuss this subject fully elsewhere.

[72] Cf., *e. g.,* Sidney Smith, *Early History of Assyria,* London, 1928, p. 233; Weissbach, *Babylonische Miscellen,* Leipzig, 1903, frontispiece and pp. 16–7; King, *Babylonian Boundary Stones,* plates 21, 54, 82, etc., Bachmann, *Felsreliefs in Assyrien,* Leipzig, 1927, *passim* (Bachmann

oddly enough regards the feather crown as a calyx). For Mitanni see the forthcoming publication of Baron von Oppenheim.

[73] Banks, *Bismya*, p. 268.

[74] Cf. Holland, *American Journal of Archæology*, 1929, p. 173 ff.; Dawkins, *Artemis Orthia*, plates 30 and 31, etc.

[75] Cf. Bossert in *Altorientalische Studien Bruno Meissner gewidmet*, Vol. II, p. 281.

[76] In illustration of this movement, we may call attention to the fact that such completely Anatolian divinities as Kubaba and Kumarbis were worshipped in Mesopotamia in the early part of the first millennium. The writer expects to discuss this question elsewhere.

[77] See Peet, *Cemeteries of Abydos* II, plate 14. One figurine has the circle of dots around the navel, together with the same bushy locks found in our figurine, and consequently is of the same type; another has the dots, but may not have the bushy locks.

[78] See Mrs. Van Buren, *Clay Figurines of Babylonia and Assyria*, New Haven, 1930, p. xlii ff.

[79] For translations see Knudtzon, *Die El-Amarna-Tafeln*, Leipzig, 1915, Nos. 279–290, 328–335, with Weber's commentary.

[80] Among the names of chieftains of these towns are good Canaanite (or Amorite) names like *Zimrida* (my protection is Adda), *Yabni-ilu, Shipti-ba'al*, Hurrian like *Pabu* (?), Indo-Iranian like *Shuwardata*.

[81] There is now a strong tendency to date the Conquest about 1400 B. C. The writer's view is that the Conquest began in the time of the Patriarchs, as described in Genesis 34, 48: 22, etc., and continued intermittently during the subsequent period, with one phase in the late sixteenth or early fifteenth century (Jericho and Ai), and a culminating triumph after the establishment of the Israelite confederation by Moses, in the second half of

the thirteenth century; cf. *Bulletin,* No. 35, p. 3 ff., and
ZAW 1929, 11 ff.

[82] The best illustration of this is that the finest palaces
and the richest tombs of the Bronze Age are unquestionably those of the Middle Bronze, contemporary with the
Hyksos period and the preceding Thirteenth Dynasty
(cir. 1800–1600 B. C.).

[83] Bribery was generally rampant among Egyptian officials, as is illustrated by the long series of court documents relative to the tomb robberies of the Twentieth
Dynasty. How bad conditions were in the Amarna age
is shown by the drastic legislation enacted by Haremhab
immediately after this period, in order to curb dishonest
tax-collectors, inspectors, and judges, and to prevent
depredations by royal officials and soldiers; see the translation by Breasted, *Ancient Records,* Vol. III, pp. 22–33.

[84] The local governors, belonging to the native nobility,
were under the supervision of Egyptian inspectors or
commissioners (*râbiṣûti*), who had mercenary garrisons,
consisting of Nubians, Arabs, and men of various Mediterranean lands. Both the officials and the mercenaries
plundered the natives, though it must be confessed that
they were frequently deprived of their due income because of corruption elsewhere in the Egyptian organization; cf. Knudtzon, Nos. 122–3, 287, etc.

[85] Cf. Knudtzon, No. 324 (Widia of Ashkelon furnishes supplies for the troops); Thureau-Dangin, *Revue
d'Assyriologie,* Vol. 19, p. 100 f. (a letter from the king
to Indaruda of Achshaph, ordering supplies for the
troops).

[86] Cf. Thureau-Dangin, *ibid.,* p. 97 f., and Alt, *Palästinajahrbuch,* Vol. 20, p. 34 ff.

[87] Pella and Rehob near Beth-shan were noted for the
manufacture of chariots (*Pap. Anastasi* 4, 16, 11 and
17, 3; cf. Max Müller, *Asien und Europa,* p. 153).

[88] See especially the letters from the prince of Jerusalem and from Shuwardata published by Knudtzon and

Thureau-Dangin.   On the Khabiru see below, p. 206, note 8.

[89] Except, of course, in Issachar and other Israelite districts under foreign domination; see Alt, *loc. cit.*

[90] Contrast I Kings 5 : 13 ff. and 11 : 28 with 9 : 20 ff.

[91] On this material see *Annual,* Vol. 4, p. 1.

[92] It is true that there is still a lack of agreement among scholars about the designation of this pottery as " Philistine," but in the writer's opinion there can no longer be any doubt that it is correct.   It is found only in the Philistine plain and the Shephelah of Judah (very rarely in Egypt and in more remote sites in southern and central Palestine) ; it does not appear before the twelfth century, when it comes in abruptly.   Finally, its closest analogies elsewhere are not in Palestine, but in Greece.

[93] Petrie's chronology is relatively excellent, but absolutely in need of a drastic revision downward; see above, p. 187, note 81.

[94] Cf. ZAW 1929, 9 f.

[95] See *Annual,* Vol. 4, pp. 11 f., 21 f.

[96] The earliest date for this occurrence is now 924 B. C. (cf. JPOS 5, 37, n. 40, where my acceptance of Schnabel's view was premature), while the latest is 917 (ZAW 1929, 9, note 3).   According to the most recent and most detailed study, that of Begrich, we should fix this date at 922 B. C. (*Die Chronologie der Könige von Israel und Juda,* 1929, p. 155).

[97] *The Excavation of Armageddon,* p. 12 ff.

[98] For the best treatment of this Gezer inscription prior to the discovery of the Byblos inscriptions see Lidzbarski, *Ephemeris,* Vol. II, p. 36 ff.   For the latest comparative table of alphabets see Dunand, RB 39, 328.

[99] Cf., *e. g.,* Jud. 6 : 2–5 ; I Sam. 30 : 1 ff.

[100] See Sellin, ZDPV 49, 232 f.; Fisher, *The Excavation of Armageddon,* p. 68.

[101] On the subject of these altars of incense, including one from Nineveh, see JPOS 9, 52 f.

[102] See Wiener, *The Altars of the Old Testament*, Leipzig, 1927; Löhr, *Das Räucheropfer im Alten Testament, eine archäologische Untersuchung*, Halle, 1927. Cf. the review JPOS 9, 50–54.

[103] *Prolegomena*, 3rd ed., p. 66 ff.; see below, p. 161.

[104] See JPOS 9, 53.

[105] It may be observed that most archæological discoveries will have a similar two-edged effect on current critical discussion. Archæology is no respecter of persons.

[106] The combination of the two elements, the dove and the function of the object, are quite sufficient to prove a relation, despite the divergence of the types otherwise.

[107] See Roscher, *Lexicon der griechischen und römischen Mythologie*, Vol. I, p. 409.

[108] Specimens of this type are found in the Cyprian collections in the British Museum, in the Metropolitan Museum, in Berlin, etc. All are of the Late Bronze Age.

[109] For a recent discussion of this type, with references to the literature, see Valentin Müller, *Frühe Plastik in Griechenland und Vorderasien*, Augsburg, 1929, p. 146 f.

[110] On the association of the dove with various goddesses see especially Gressmann, *Archiv für Religionswissenschaft*, Vol. 20, pp. 332–59.

[111] For the nature of this symbolism see the observation in *Archiv für Orientforschung*, Vol. 5, p. 119 b.

[112] The center of the cult of the dove-goddess was precisely at Ashkelon, less than two days' journey from Tell Beit Mirsim; see especially Gressmann, *loc. cit.*

[113] As has been observed above, Petrie, *Gerar*, passim, has placed the introduction of iron into everyday use more than a century too early. Iron did not come into general use in Egypt until the Bubastite period, some two centuries later than in Palestine.

Since they are apparently not found at all in Egypt it would seem that they must come from Phœnicia originally.

[130] The Hebrew name for this substance is *pûk* (used, *e. g.*, by Jezebel, II Kings 9:30), but it was also called *kuḥl*, written *gukhlu* in cuneiform (Haupt, *Orientalistische Literaturzeitung*, 1913, col. 492 f.); Hezekiah included it in his tribute to Sennacherib (B. C. 701).

[131] For the identification of stibium, Egyptian *mesdemet*, see Lucas, *Ancient Egyptian Materials*, London, 1926, p. 146 f. Sulphide of lead was also used in Egypt. Extensive deposits of manganese occur in Midian and Edom; it was presumably from there that Hezekiah secured his oxide of manganese (if this identification is correct in this case).

[132] Cf. Erman-Ranke, *Ægypten*, p. 257.

[133] *Ibid.*, p. 258.

[134] Our hearty thanks are due to Dean J. A. Huffman of Marion, Indiana, who was particularly successful in rescuing inscribed potsherds.

[135] These inscriptions read: [ל]גרא, לחזק[י]ן, לעז[י]ו, לנ[חם].

[136] See JPOS 5, 45 ff.

[137] JPOS 5, 52; Alt, *Palästinajahrbuch*, Vol. 25, p. 86 f.

[138] JPOS 5, 53. It is true, of course, that the flying roll of Zechariah was apparently spread open, not rolled up, but this is no serious objection to the explanation. The object on the seals is cylindrical, with both ends bulging, like a roll.

[139] לאליקם נער יוכן, *i. e.*, *le-Elyaqîm naʿar Yaukîn* (as the name *Yôkîn* was then pronounced). For a philological discussion see provisionally ZAW 1929, 16, and my forthcoming article in JBL.

[140] For details see the forthcoming paper in JBL, already referred to. It may be said here that the use of the terms *ʿebed*, " servant," and *naʿar*, " steward," on

important seals is restricted to royal officials; see for
'ebed the full discussions by Clermont-Ganneau, *Recueil
d'archéologie orientale*, Vol. I, p. 33 ff.; Kautzsch,
*Mitteilungen und Nachrichten des Deutschen Palästina-
Vereins*, 1904, p. 1 ff.; Lidzbarski, *Ephemeris*, Vol. II,
p. 142 ff.; Torrey, *Annual*, Vol. II/III, p. 104 f. All
these eminent scholars agree absolutely in this view of
the use of *'ebed* on seals from Palestine. The word
na'ar is employed primarily of any youth, then of a
personal attendant, and finally of a steward who is
placed over someone's property or estate; cf. II Kings
4 : 12, 5 : 20, Ruth 2 : 15, etc. The clearest case is that
of Ziba (II Sam. 9 : 9, 16 : 1, 19 : 18), who is called the
"steward (*na'ar*) of Saul" and the "steward of the
house of Saul." Even after Saul's death Ziba appears
in this capacity, and after Meribaal (*Mephibosheth*)
receives the usufruct of the estate, it continues to be
administered by Ziba. The importance of the latter is
illustrated by the statement that he had fifteen sons and
twenty slaves. It may be supposed that Eliakim was
the intendant in charge of the personal (crown) property of Joiachin, and that he remained in this capacity
after the exile of the latter. Our seals can hardly date
from the three months of Joiachin's actual reign, during
the siege of Jerusalem.

[141] II Kings 24 : 8 ff., Jer. 13 : 18 f., etc.

[142] Joiachin's return was confidently expected by the
people: Jer. 28 : 1–4; cf. Jer. 24. The exiles in Babylonia continued to date by his regnal years: Ezek. 1 : 2,
II Kings 25 : 27, etc. The dynasty was continued in his
line, though none of his descendants ever occupied a
position of importance in Judah except Sheshbazzar
(Sanabassar) and Zerubbabel.

NOTES ON CHAPTER III

[1] See Wellhausen, *Prolegomena,* 3rd ed., p. 331.

[2] The change is particularly noticeable in Germany, where the growing opposition to Wellhausenism, though generally with full recognition of the importance of Wellhausen's own contribution, centers around the extremely influential school of Kittel. The latter gave expression to his point of view regarding Wellhausenism in the following pungent words, spoken in his address at the first German Alttestamentlertag, which was held at Leipzig in 1921 (ZAW 1921, 86) : " Es fehlte dem Gebäude das Fundament, und es fehlten den Baumeistern die Massstäbe," *i. e.,* The structure (of the Wellhausen school) lacked a foundation, and the builders were without measuring rods.

[3] Sayce and Hommel are neither strictly conservative, as is sometimes supposed; their views depart far enough at times from traditional lines. Both are characterized by an originality which generally overshoots the mark, so that very few of their innumerable observations have stood the test of time. Winckler represents an entirely different point of view. He was the real founder of the astral-mythological or pan-Babylonian school, once very influential, but now almost extinct; Alfred Jeremias is the only active living exponent of it. Winckler, however, possessed marked philosophical ability, and he was the first to understand the nature of the oral transmission of history, and to recognize that it is quite possible for a given element to be history and folklore at the same time.

[4] This brochure is the expanded form of his article in the new edition of the *Encyclopædia Britannica,* Vol. I, p. 59 f.

[5] *Op. cit.,* p. 73.

[6] Beit Feddjâr is the village nearest the site of Tekoa,

the home of Amos. It is interesting to note that a similar environment forced Amos to spend part of the year abroad as a hired labourer.

[7] There is no reason to doubt the common view that the Kenites (*Qênîm* from *qain, qên,* " smith ") were travelling coppersmiths, especially since their original home was in Sinai and Midian, where copper mines had been worked from the earliest times. While in some respects analogous to the modern gypsies (Náwar or Zuṭṭ) of Palestine, as well as to the Ṣleib in Arabia (see especially Werner Pieper, *Le Monde Orientale,* Vol. 17 [1923], pp. 1–75), the social position of the Kenites was undoubtedly much superior. The smith enjoyed a much greater prestige then than now.

[8] The Khabiru problem grows more complicated all the time. The material has been discussed recently by Jirku, *Die Wanderungen der Hebräer,* Leipzig, 1924, and by Landsberger, *Kleinasiatische Forschungen,* Vol. I, pp. 321–34 (1929), among others. The writer's views are developed JBL 43, 389–92, and JAOS 48, 183–5; he agrees, quite independently, with Landsberger's view that the term *Khabiru* means " condottiere, condottieri." It is now probable that the word is an appellative, like its synonym *khabbatu,* " raider, bandit," as maintained by Landsberger. The way in which the Khabiru are described in the Amarna letters makes it probable that the same people are referred to in the broken Sethos stele of Beth-shan, line 10, where the name is spelled *'Apiru,* written with determinatives meaning " foreign warriors." Since the cuneiform orthography *Kha-BI-ru* may just as well be read *Khapiru* and Canaanite *'ain* is regularly transcribed *kh* in the Amarna tablets, it is difficult to avoid the conclusion that the true form of the name is *'Apiru.* Hebrew *'Eber,* for *'Ibr, 'Ipr* (which is derived from *'Apir* in the same way that late Canaanite *milk,* " king," is derived from older *malik,* " prince ") is then presumably a specifically Hebrew form with

partial assimilation, as in the word *hopshî,* " peasant freeholder," for Canaanite *(awîl) khubshî,* " peasant (bound to the soil)," etc. The relation between the collective *'Ibr* and the gentilic *'Ibrî* is exactly that between *khubshu* and *hopshî.* The sense " condottiere " was early lost, and has left no trace in the classical Hebrew use of the name. Khabiru names mentioned in the cuneiform inscriptions belong to several languages, and there is no reason to believe that the designation was then peculiar to a single ethnic group. The form *'Apiru,* if correct, suggests a Canaanite or Amorite origin, and the name may have belonged originally (*i. e.,* in very early times) to some nomadic group like the Midianite tribe of the same name (Gen. 25:4). The writer expects to discuss this complicated subject elsewhere at length.

[9] While the German excavations have not yet disclosed the building level of MB I, sherds from this period have been found in abundance in the lowest stratum. Shechem is mentioned in an Egyptian inscription of the nineteenth century B. C. (JPOS 8, 226 f.; 233).

[10] See *Bulletin,* No. 29, p. 10.

[11] The pottery of et-Tell (Ai) covers the latter part of EB, all MB (apparently), and the beginning of LB; cf. ZAW 1929, 12.

[12] Cf. *Jewish Quarterly Review,* Vol. 21 (1930), 165 f.

[13] See Petrie, *Gerar,* London, 1928, and Hempel, ZAW 1929, 63 f. Isolated Middle Bronze sherds were found in the excavation.

[14] Middle Bronze sherds occur on the slopes of the mound.

[15] Beersheba is not certain; the writer has not actually found any pottery antedating the Early Iron on Tell el-Imshâsh. Yet the mound is fairly high, and many of the mounds in the Negeb go back to the Middle Bronze or earlier, so an MB date for Beersheba must be considered probable.

[16] On the hill er-Rumeideh, just above the town, are the cyclopæan walls of an ancient town, which apparently was never occupied, to judge from the absence of early pottery. The Bronze Age mound lies presumably under the modern town in the valley.

[17] In the story of Judah (Gen. 38), the town of Adullam is mentioned. While this story may not belong to the primary patriarchal cycle, it is curious to find that Adullam was also occupied during the Age of the Patriarchs. On a visit to its site, modern Khirbet esh-Sheikh Madhkûr, with Garstang, in 1928, we picked up several characteristic sherds from the Middle Bronze, both MB I and MB II, at the foot of the mound.

[18] See *Geschichte des Altertums,* Vol. II, 1, 2nd ed., p. 96.

[19] See *Bulletin,* No. 14; *Annual,* Vol. VI, pp. 56 ff.; Mallon in *Biblica,* Vol. 5, pp. 413–55. A very interesting popular account is given by Kyle in his book *Explorations at Sodom,* New York, 1928. The full report of our expedition is in course of preparation.

[20] See especially *Biblica,* 1929, p. 95 ff., 214 ff.; 1930, p. 3 ff.

[21] For the latter see Father Power in *Biblica,* 1930, pp. 23–62. The pottery from Tuleilât el-Ghassûl is characteristically chalcolithic; see above, p. 62. The site was abandoned at least a thousand years before the time of Abraham.

[22] See *Annual,* Vol. VI, p. 54, with the references there given to the work of Schwöbel and Schroetter.

[23] This date is fixed absolutely by the pottery from the site, great quantities of which have been examined by the writer on different visits. The description of the pottery has been awaiting publication for some time. It may be observed that the latest pottery from Bâb ed-Drâ‘ is older than the G period at Tell Beit Mirsim; the settlement was abandoned early in our I—H period.

[24] See the regular reports which have appeared in the

Bulletin, Nos. 18–42, and *Annual,* Vol. VI, pp. 75–92 (Chiera and Speiser), Vol. X, 1–73 (Speiser); Koschaker, *Neue keilschriftliche Rechtsurkunden aus der el-Amarna-Zeit,* Leipzig, 1928. Three volumes of tablets from this site have been published already by Chiera (besides two respectable collections published by Contenau and by Gadd).

[25] Gen. 15 : 2. It is generally recognized that the derivation of Eliezer from Damascus is very doubtful, being probably an ancient gloss explaining the obscure work *mesheq.*

[26] See *Revue d'Assyriologie,* Vol. 23 (1928), pp. 126–7, and Speiser, *Mesopotamian Origins,* Philadelphia, 1930, p. 162.

[27] It must be said that the antiquity of the tradition deriving Abraham from Ur of the Chaldees is very doubtful, since there were no Chaldæans in Babylonia before the end of the second millennium, while the LXX renders simply "in the land of the Chaldæans," thus presupposing a slightly different consonantal text in 11 : 28, 31. The absence of the name from the Greek translation of the third century B. C. is in any case very remarkable. It has sometimes been suggested that both the Hebrew and the Greek texts reflect a different original, which may have referred to Arphaxad (Gen. 11 : 10 ff.), since the Hebrew consonants are nearly the same.

[28] The original form of the name is probably not *Abîrâm* (my father is exalted), as maintained, *e. g.,* by Gunkel in his commentary, but *Abamrâm* (exalted with respect to father—see JBL 37, 133, n. 21), a West-Semitic personal name found in a cuneiform tablet of the nineteenth century B. C. from Babylonia (Ungnad, *Beiträge zur Assyriologie,* Vol. 6, part 5, p. 60). The old explanation of the name as simply *Ab-ram,* "Exalted Father" (taken by Eduard Meyer to be a divine appellation) is certainly wrong.

[29] For these names see especially the discussion JBL 43, 385 ff. Explanations were here offered for *Peleg* and *Reu* as well as for these three certain cases. The explanation offered for *Reu* is very doubtful, but the identification of the name *Peleg* with the name of the town of Phaliga on the Euphrates, just above the mouth of the Khabûr, is quite certain. The town in question is mentioned in a parchment recently dug up at Dura-Europus, as *Paliga* (Baur and Rostovtzeff, *The Excavations at Dura-Europos,* New Haven, 1931, pp. 206–7). The spelling *Phalga* occurs elsewhere. Identity of name does not, in this case, prove that the patriarch Peleg is to be connected directly with the town.

[30] For *Arphaxad* cf. JBL 37, 134–6; 43, 388 f. While the problem is in a way no less obscure than it was before, the explanation of the *shad* ending as being the Accadian (Assyrian) word for "mountains, east" is undoubtedly made easier by the parallel *Tirqan-shadî,* "eastern Tirqan" (JAOS 45, 222 f.), especially since the latter place was in the vicinity of the probable location of the former (supposed to be Arrapkha, modern Kirkûk and its environs).

[31] See Burrows, *Journal of the Royal Asiatic Society,* 1925, p. 281 ff.

[32] For the exact location of Mount Nizir (Niṣir) see now Speiser, *Annual,* Vol. VIII, p. 18 f. The identification of Nizir with the impressive peak of Pir Omar Gudrun appears to be certain.

[33] This is so well known that no discussion is needed; cf. Olympus, Harā Berezaiti of the Iranians, Meru of the Indians, the *har mô'ed* of Ezekiel, etc. For the rôle played by Khashur-Kashiari, the *Masius mons* of the Romans, cf. AJSL 35, 179 ff.

[34] See AJSL 36, 280 ff.; 39, 15 ff. The place-name in question is the well-known *Beth-eden* (*Bit-adini*) of the Upper Euphrates valley. The difference in vocalization is, in any case, due to a later differentiation.

[35] See JSOR 1926, 263, endorsed by Gressmann, ZAW 1926, 290.

[36] Albright, JSOR 1926, 231–69; Böhl, *Das Zeitalter Abrahams* (see above).

[37] For this date see Thureau-Dangin, *Revue d'Assyriologie*, Vol. 24, pp. 181–98 (1927). Weidner's date, 1758 B. C., is increasingly accepted by historians, and may well be correct. The writer long opposed the low chronology of the First Dynasty of Babylon, but now accepts it, though at the same time he lowers the date for the beginning of the Third Dynasty of Babylon by a century or more. He accepts to write again on this subject soon.

[38] See Gustavs, *Die Personennamen in den Tontafeln von Tell Ta'annek*, Leipzig, 1928, pp. 57 f., 26 f. The writer's defense of the earlier date, awaited by Gustavs, has not appeared because of his inability to collate the originals owing to the absence of the responsible museum officials during a visit to Constantinople for the purpose.

[39] See *Archiv für Orientforschung*, Vol. 6, p. 221 (1931) on Yahuda, *Die Sprache des Pentateuchs*, p. 282, who first suggested the combination.

[40] *Bulletin*, No. 35, p. 10. For the original identification cf. JSOR 10, 260, and Steuernagel, *Zeitschrift des Deutschen Palästina-Vereins*, 1925, p. 79.

[41] Cf. also Jirku, *Zeitschrift des Deutschen Palästina-Vereins*, 1930, p. 151 f.

[42] *Bulletin*, No. 35, p. 10 ff.

[43] *Bulletin*, No. 14, 10; the writer hopes to publish a report on the early temple discovered at Ader in the near future.

[44] The importance of the copper deposits in Seir (Edom) was discovered by Musil, and the ancient mines have been studied recently by Blake and others, on behalf of the Transjordan government. The copper and gold of Midian, and especially the copper of Sinai (for which see

Petrie, *Researches in Sinai,* London, 1906) have long been known. Manganese occurs in large quantities southeast of Edom. An engineer who was engaged in studying the deposits of manganese in this region showed me a fine scarab of the Saite period which he had picked up there (1930). That the Egyptians were interested in finding sources of manganese (*mesdemet*) is well known, but it was not suspected that they secured it from this region. It was evidently from this region that the Jewish king Hezekiah secured the manganese (*kuḥl*) which he gave as tribute to Sennacherib (see above, p. 203, n. 130).

[45] Cf. Gunkel, *Genesis,* 4th ed., p. 438 f., with the references there given to Spiegelberg's discussions of the names.

[46] The writer hopes to discuss this question in full elsewhere.

[47] For the explanation of the name *Ya'qob-har* see already JBL 37 (1918), p. 137, n. 24; the element *har,* "mountain," must be taken as a divine name like *Ṣûr,* "mountain," and *Shaddai,* and the name rendered " Har protects." The divine name in question will be discussed elsewhere in the light of some very early West-Semitic occurrences. As is well known, the name *Jacob* stands for *Ya'qob-el,* " God protects." The parallel Hyksos name *'Anati-har* is like Biblical Hebrew *'Antôti-yah,* which means approximately " Yahweh is my providence."

[48] For scarabs of Ḥûr, with his title, see Petrie, *Scarabs and Cylinders,* plate xvii, BT–CE; the spelling Ḥa-al is naturally wrong.

[49] See especially Eduard Meyer, *Geschichte,* Vol. I, 3rd ed., p. 318 ff.

[50] See *Zeitschrift für Ægyptische Sprache,* Vol. 65 (1930), pp. 85–9.

[51] See, *e. g.,* Bury in the *Cambridge Ancient History,* Vol. II, p. 510 ff., and Eduard Meyer, *Geschichte,* Vol. II, 1, 2nd ed., p. 288 ff.

[52] See especially Wüst, *Wiener Zeitschrift für die Kunde des Morgenlandes*, Vol. 34 (1927), pp. 164–215.

[53] See especially Burney, *The Book of Judges;* Haupt, *Studien zur semitischen Philologie (Wellhausen Festschrift)*, Giessen, 1914, p. 191 ff.; Albright, JPOS 2, 69 ff.; Morgenstern, *Jewish Quarterly Review*, Vol. 9 (1918–9), p. 359 ff.

[54] Sievers has gone even farther, attempting to scan entire prose narratives as verse. However far-fetched his attempt may seem, there can be no doubt that the discoverer of Schallanalyse possesses a marvelous feeling for rhythm, which enables him to detect it even when disguised.

[55] Löhr has shown (*Orientalistische Literaturzeitung*, 1928, col. 923 ff.) that "rider" is entirely wrong; see also Albright, *Archiv für Orientforschung*, Vol. 6, p. 220.

[56] A satisfactory treatment of the Song of Balaam remains to be given, though perhaps at present quite impossible. Mowinckel's effort (ZAW 1930, 233 ff.) cannot be considered successful, though very much better than von Gall's (*Zusammensetzung der Bileamperikope*, Giessen, 1900). The latter, followed by others, dates the end of the Balaam prophecies in the Greek period.

[57] See Kittel, *Geschichte*, Vol. I (5–6th ed.), pp. 260, 340.

[58] *Das Zeitalter Abrahams*, Leipzig, 1930, pp. 1 ff., 31 ff.

[59] The writer has long been convinced that the dates given by the Wellhausen school (and *a fortiori* the dates of Sellin and Ed. König) for the redaction in writing of J and E are too high—considerably too high in the former case. A careful study of Genesis X and other passages in the light of our present knowledge is decisive in this respect. It was precisely the fall of Samaria that aroused a greater interest in the past history of Israel

among the literary circles of Judah. J and E must follow the height of the prophetic movement, not precede it.

[60] Cf. Meyer, *Geschichte*, Vol. II, 1, 2nd ed., p. 288 ff.

[61] Yahuda's attempt to prove a profound Egyptian influence on the Pentateuch (*Die Sprache des Pentateuchs in ihren Beziehungen zum Ægyptischen*, Berlin, 1929) is a complete failure, despite some few correct and stimulating observations; see the reviews by Spiegelberg and Bergsträsser, *Zeitschrift für Semitistik*, Vol. 7, 113–23; 8, 1–40, as well as by the writer in *Kirjath Sepher*, Vol. 6 (1929), pp. 195–6 (Hebrew). A fanciful attempt to establish the existence of an Egyptian stream of Hebrew tradition has been made by Luria (ZAW, 1926, 94 ff.).

[62] This view is now accepted by practically all Biblical historians, both liberal and conservative. For the writer's view cf. provisionally ZAW 1929, 11 ff.; *Bulletin*, No. 35, 3 ff.

[63] Cf. JBL 37, 111 ff.; May, AJSL 47, 83 ff.

[64] Cf. JPOS 1, 51 ff.

[65] For the combination of historical and mythical elements in the story of Semiramis see especially Lehmann-Haupt, *Klio*, Vol. 15, p. 243 ff.; *Die historische Semiramis und ihre Zeit*, Tübingen, 1910. Semiramis became more and more fused with Ishtar, until all historical basis of the popular account of her life vanished. Queen Stratonice, consort of Antiochus Soter, had nearly the same posthumous experience more than five centuries later (cf. JBL 37, 126 ff. and *Archiv für Orientforschung*, 5, 230 f.).

[66] See Wellhausen, *Geschichte*, 7th ed., p. 15 ff.

[67] The best edition of the laws of Hammurabi is Kohler and Ungnad, *Hammurabi's Gesetz*, Leipzig, 1909 ff. The most recent independent translation is given by Ebeling in AOTB I, 380–410. For the latest and best comparative treatment of the Babylonian laws, as well as of the Assyrian and Hittite legislation, see

Edouard Cuq, *Études sur le droit babylonien, les lois assyriennes et les lois hittites,* Paris, 1929.

[68] The latest and best detailed treatment is given by Ehelolf and Koschaker, *Ein altassyrisches Rechtsbuch,* Berlin, 1922. The most recent independent translation is that of Ebeling, AOTB I, 412–22.

[69] See Zimmern and Friedrich, *Hethitische Gesetze,* Leipzig, 1922; Hrozny, *Code hittite provenant de l'Asie Mineure,* Paris, 1922; Ebeling, AOTB I, 423–31.

[70] *Les origines cananéennes du sacrifice israélite,* Paris, 1921. Cf. Lods, *Éléments anciens et éléments modernes dans le rituel du sacrifice israélite,* in *Revue d'Histoire et de Philosophie Religieuses,* Vol. 8 (1928), pp. 399 ff.

[71] Cf. especially his book *Das weltliche Recht im Alten Testament,* Gütersloh, 1927, and his paper *Das israelitische Jobeljahr* in *Reinhold Seeberg-Festschrift,* Vol. II, p. 169 ff.

[72] Despite the cumulative evidence, we still lack the material from Phœnician sources to explain the Temple of Solomon in detail. For some northern influences on the cult furnishings of the Temple see JBL 39, p. 137 ff.

[73] The reference to the bringing in of horses and chariots becomes much more vivid in the light of recent discoveries at Megiddo, described in chapter I. Chariots and horses were evidently still looked upon with suspicion when the nucleus of Deuteronomy was composed.

[74] See Driver, *Introduction,* 6th ed., p. 97 f.

[75] The iron mines of Lebanon were operated in the time of Nabonidus in the sixth century B. C., as we know from a tablet published by Dougherty, *Records from Erech, Time of Nabonidus,* New Haven, 1920, No. 168. That iron had been previously exploited by the Phœnicians to whom Mount Lebanon belonged may be considered as certain.

[76] See especially Welch, *The Code of Deuteronomy,* 1924. The question of Deuteronomy has recently been

discussed in a symposium by Bewer, Paton and Dahl, JBL 1928, 305–79.

[77] Sellin and Noth (see his book *Das System der zwölf Stämme Israels,* 1930) maintain that Shechem possessed this significance for Israel at an even earlier date. In view of the semi-Canaanite character of Shechem until about 1100 (time of Abimelech) this seems improbable.

[78] See Morgenstern, *The Book of the Covenant,* Cincinnati, 1928 (also in *Hebrew Union College Annual,* Vol. V.).

[79] JPOS 5, 20 ff.

[80] *Prolegomena,* 3rd ed., pp. 40, 43; *Geschichte,* 7th ed., p. 50.

[81] *Geschichte,* 7th ed., p. 50.

[82] Cf. Benzinger, *Archäologie,* 3rd ed., p. 107, and Grant's forthcoming Beth-shemesh volume. The horizontal position of the lights was retained.

[83] See Noth, *Das System der zwölf Stämme Israels,* Stuttgart, 1930, *passim,* and Alt, *Die Staatenbildung der Israeliten in Palästina,* Leipzig, 1930, p. 10 ff.

[84] In this connection attention should be called to the instructive discussion of the tent-shrine in Israel, with particular reference to Mizpah and Gibeon, by Hertzberg, ZAW 1929, especially pp. 166–77.

[85] Cf. Haupt, *Midian und Sinai, Zeitschrift der Deutschen Morgenländischen Gesellschaft,* Vol. 63 (1909), p. 506 ff., especially p. 514.

[86] See his exhaustive treatment of the theological sources of the Aton conception in his *Beiträge zur Geschichte Amenophis' IV (Nachrichten v. d. Kön. Ges. d. Wiss. z. Göttingen, Phil.-hist. Klasse,* 1921, 2), and his brilliant study of the origin and development of the Heliopolitan theological system in his *Urgeschichte und älteste Religion der Ægypter,* Leipzig, 1930.

[87] See JBL 43, 370 ff., where the writer failed to grasp the rather obvious fact that this formula is actually the

full form of the divine name, and that *Yahwêh* is an abbreviation. Abbreviated divine names were very common in the ancient Orient, especially among the Sumerians, where we have, *e. g., Damu* for *Du(a)mu-zid-abzu, Shagan* for *Ama-shagan-gub*, etc. In Egypt personal names were very greatly abbreviated in every-day use, and the same is probably true of divine names. In Israel we also have illustrations; the most striking are the names of the two " pillars " before the Temple of Solomon, Jachin and Boaz, whose names the writer has long considered abbreviations of some such formulæ as " He who creates what exists " and " In Him alone is strength (or help)." It may be added that the numerous recent attempts to explain *Yah* and *Yáhû* as older than *Yahwêh*, and to cast doubt on the latter pronunciation are absolutely without etymological or historical parallel, whereas there are perfectly satisfactory explanations of all the reduced forms. Besides the paper in JBL 43, 370 ff. see JBL 44, 158 ff., and especially JBL 46, 175 ff. In support of the originality of the form *Yahwêh* see further Noth, *Die israelitischen Personennamen*, Stuttgart, 1928, p. 101 ff.

[88] See JBL 43, 378.

[89] See Theo. Bauer, *Die Ostkanaanäer*, Leipzig, 1926, especially p. 74 a, where he derives the element variously written *Yakhwi* and *Yawi* correctly from *Yahwî*.

[90] There is some doubt with regard to the latter name, for which see Tallqvist, *Assyrian Personal Names, ad voc.*

[91] For a translation of this text see Ebeling, AOTB 329.

[92] For these gods see especially the oath formula of the treaty between Suppiluliuma of Khatte and Mattiwaza of Mitanni.

[93] This designation of the principal deity first appears in the treaty between Suppiluliuma and Mattiwaza, in Accadian (Assyrian) dress, as *Bêl shamê*.

[94] See AJSL 41, 84, 88, 90. On the principle of the use of a plural of names of divinities in a collective sense see further Kittel, *Geschichte,* Vol. I (5th and 6th ed.), p. 173.

[95] It cannot be emphasized too strongly that the prophetic movement was a religious and social reformation, and not a creative movement in the primary sense. It should rather be compared to the Protestant reformation of the sixteenth century and the corresponding Wahhâbī movement in Islam. Like these movements it eschewed elaboration of ritual; there was also a strongly marked tendency to return to the simple life of the forefathers; cf. Flight's paper " The Nomadic Idea and Ideal in the Old Testament," JBL 42, 158–226.

[96] See *Zeitschrift der Deutschen Morgenländischen Gesellschaft,* 1927, p. xlvii.

[97] So Torrey in his brilliant books *Ezra Studies* (Chicago, 1910) and *The Second Isaiah* (New York, 1928). Somewhat similar views are held by Stanley Cook and Hölscher. The writer believes that Torrey's reasoning is entirely sound, but that his premises are wrong. He has shown that the Ezra memoirs are written by the hand of the Chronicler; the writer maintains that Ezra was the Chronicler (JBL 40, 104 ff.). He has proved convincingly that Deutero-Isaiah and Trito-Isaiah are one, a conclusion which leads him to date this work in the latter part of the fifth century, and to excise references to Cyrus as glosses; the writer, with a different reconstruction of the history of the Restoration, would date the work 540–522 B. C. (in round numbers).

[98] This view has been ably defended by the Flemish scholar of Louvain, A. Van Hoonacker, in numerous books and articles (the latest, a reply to Kugler's criticisms, is found in *Revue Biblique,* 1923, 481 ff.; 1924, 33 ff.), and is accepted by the École Biblique in Jerusalem. Other weighty protagonists are Batten, *Ezra and Nehemiah* (*International Critical Commentary*), New

York, 1913, and Bertholet, *Die Bücher Esra und Nehemia*, Tübingen, 1902, who follows Kosters, *Die Wiederherstellung Israels*, Heidelberg, 1895, p. 63 ff. The writer defended Van Hoonacker's view JBL 40, 104 ff., but now favours the date of Bertholet and Kosters (cir. 430 B. C., about the thirty-second year of Artaxerxes I). The chronological details in Ezra and Nehemiah are corrupt, and Josephus' data may be more correct—the latter's statement of the duration of the building of the wall of Jerusalem is certainly preferable to that of our present Biblical text. It may be observed that Rothstein and Hänel, in their new commentary in two volumes on the First Book of Chronicles, date the first compilation of the Chronicler's work in the late fifth century, a date which seems to the writer quite correct, though nearly half a century earlier than he would have dared to place it before. This whole subject will be discussed in detail elsewhere, in the light of new material.

[99] See the historical sketch given JBL 40, 104 ff.

[100] Sachau, *Drei aramäische Papyrusurkunden aus Elephantine*, Berlin, 1907 (*Abh. d. Kön. Preuss. Akad. d. Wiss., Phil.-hist. Klasse*).

[101] Sachau, *Aramäische Papyrus und Ostraka*, Leipzig, 1911. The latest complete translation and commentary on the papyri is given by Cowley, *Aramaic Papyri of the Fifth Century B. C.*, Oxford, 1923.

[102] See Causse, *Les dispersés d'Israel*, Paris, 1929.

[103] See Eduard Meyer, *Der Papyrusfund von Elephantine*, Leipzig, 1912, p. 70 ff.; Hölscher, in Kautzsch, *Heilige Schrift des Alten Testaments*, 4th ed., p. 525; Albright, *loc. cit.* Torrey's opposition to this view of the chronology (JBL 47, 380 ff.) is due to the fact that he refuses to admit the authenticity of the references to the high-priest Eliashib, Neh. 3:1; 13:28, and elsewhere, which alone prove that Nehemiah was the contemporary of the grandfather of Johanan, who was

high-priest in the years 411 and 408. The Sanballat of Nehemiah must then be Sanballat I and not Sanballat II, the contemporary of Alexander the Great. I was, of course, quite wrong in trying to identify the father of Nicaso and father-in-law of Manasseh with the father of Delaiah and Shelemiah (JBL 40, 124), since Nicaso is, after all, a good Greek name, and the circumstantial narrative of Josephus with regard to the relations between her father and Alexander should not be treated so lightly.

[104] This was stated emphatically by Eduard Meyer, *Entstehung des Judentums,* pp. 70–1, and triumphantly confirmed by him, *Papyrusfund,* pp. 96–7. Few scholars have been so fortunate in having their brilliant historical deductions confirmed by further archæological discoveries as Eduard Meyer was.

[105] On this subject cf. AJSL 41, 92 ff.; 41, 283 ff.; 43, 233 ff. The previous literature is referred to in these discussions; for a recent independent study see Noth, *Die israelitischen Personennamen,* p. 122 ff. The writer now has much additional material in support of his thesis that the triad of divinities worshipped by the Jews of Elephantine are properly abstract hypostases of ultimately pagan origin.

[106] So maintained by the writer, JBL 40, 113 ff. There are three excellent recent studies of the language of the Aramaic of Ezra: Baumgartner, ZAW 1927, 81 ff. (see especially p. 120 ff.); Rowley, *The Aramaic of the Old Testament,* Oxford, 1929; Charles, *Daniel,* Oxford, 1929. The best is still that of Baumgartner, in the writer's opinion. It may be observed that no certain conclusion can be reached from the orthography of the consonants, and that Rowley's humorous remarks anent Daniel as a spelling reformer are out of place. To the student of the ancient Orient it is a commonplace that texts were being revised grammatically as well as orthographically at all periods. That this process was carried on in the

Old Testament is absolutely certain, especially since we now know that the language of the Northern Kingdom (*i. e.*, of E and of all portions of the Bible which originated there) was quite different from Biblical Hebrew, and that the vowel-letters were all introduced into the text after the Exile. It is quite certain that the Aramaic of Ezra is rather later than that of the Elephantine papyri, and that the Aramaic of Daniel is perceptibly later than the language of Ezra. But the *lingua franca* of the Persian Empire most certainly did not change materially between the end of the sixth century and the early third century B. C. That the Aramaic of Daniel is later than the middle of the third century is most improbable, and the Aramaic of Ezra may perfectly well go back to the end of the fifth century or the beginning of the fourth.

[107] *Entstehung des Judentums,* p. 8 ff. The latest attempt to prove the existence of a Greek word in Ezra is by Cowley, *Journal of Theological Studies,* Vol. 30 (1929), p. 54 ff., where Ar. *pithgama* is very cleverly combined with Greek *epitagma,* " order, command." In a number of passages this meaning will not fit at all. Cowley accuses all scholars of following blindly after Gildemeister, who proposed a Persian etymology for this word in 1842, but he has surely overlooked the fact that Andreas (whose judgment was certainly independent!) endorsed and restated this etymology in his note in Marti, *Kurzgefasste Grammatik der biblisch-armäischen Sprache,* 2nd ed., Berlin, 1911, p. 87*b.

[108] For a complete account of this discovery, with full literature, and an elaborate discussion, see the remarkable article by Vincent, *Revue Biblique,* 1920, pp. 161–202.

[109] Cf. Vincent, *op. cit.,* and Gressmann, *Die ammonitischen Tobiaden,* Berlin, 1921 (*Sitz. Berl. Akad. Wiss.*).

[110] That the Tobiad family became Persianized at an

early date is certain from the family name Hyrcanus (Persian *Vurkâniya, Vurkân*), borne by the last of the line, who died about 175 B. C. For the Persian noble family of the Hyrcanians (*Vurkâniyân*) see F. W. König in the *Wiener Zeitschrift für die Kunde des Morgenlandes,* Vol. 33, pp. 23–56. In a similar way it may be proved that the house of Sanballat ascended into the Assyrian period, the seventh century B. C.; see JBL 40, III, n. 17.

[111] For an exhaustive palæographic study of the inscription see Vincent, JPOS 3, 55 ff. Vincent dates it in the third century, assigning it to Tobiah II. A date about 400 B. C., and an identification with Tobiah I is perhaps equally possible, since the Aramaic script changed but little during the Persian period.

[112] Such confusion as exists is only in the minds of scholars who have not followed the post-War development of Palestinian ceramics, on which see chapter I.

[113] We hope to secure additional evidence in the excavation of the site of Beth-zur, which was occupied certainly both before and after the Exile.

[114] I Esdras 5 : 2, 6. For the critical problems involved in this passage see Bewer, AJSL 36, 18 ff., and Torrey, AJSL 37, 81 ff.

[115] *Geschichte,* Vol. 3, 2, p. 319 ff.

[116] *Entstehung des Judentums,* p. 94 ff.; *Geschichte,* Vol. 3, 2, p. 330 ff.

[117] For Sheshbazzar-Sanabassar-Sinabuṣur and his identity with Shenazzar see JBL 40, 108 ff. To be exact one should write *Shinabuṣur.*

[118] *Op. cit.,* p. 468.

[119] *Mitteilungen der Vorderasiatisch-ægyptischen Gesellschaft,* Vol. 35, 1, pp. 1, 5.

[120] JPOS 6, 93 ff.

[121] Hebrew עֲדָיָה.

[122] Hebrew יְדַעְיָה, reading the *yôd* twice.

[123] Ezra 2 : 26 = Neh. 7 : 39. In the list of the priestly

orders given in I Chron. 24 : 7 ff. Jedaiah is second, the primacy falling to Joiarib, the order of the Hasmonæan house, but the change is due to a later scribe.

[124] The spelling שלמין is strictly on a par with the archaizing of the script. Irregularities in the appearance of the characters in different impressions show that the archaism was sometimes attempted without success, just as in the case of later Jewish coins.

[125] For the *Yah* and *Yahu* stamps see also Vincent, JPOS 3, 64. It may be added that the writer has seen stamps with this inscription which have been picked up at Jericho, so that the number recorded by Sellin and Watzinger must be increased. Additional stamps have been found by Garstang during his excavations on the site.

ADDENDA

P. 54. On the first campaign at Tell el-'Addjûl see now Petrie, *Ancient Egypt,* 1931, p. 33 ff.

P. 142. Mr. G. Horsfield, Director of Antiquities in Transjordan, has carefully explored the region of eastern Moab and Edom, with most extraordinary results, which were described by him at the Leyden Congress of Orientalists, in September, 1931 (see provisionally *Bulletin,* No. 43, p. 21 f.). He has found numerous sites which were occupied during the Bronze Age, especially during the first half of the second millennium. At several sites he found great masses of copper slag. The settlements at Khirbet Bālû'ah and el-Lehûn, near the upper course of the Arnon, were abandoned during the Bronze Age, after having been very prosperous. In the summer of 1931 the writer continued his study of the ancient sites of eastern Transjordan, and found several important settlements of the Early and Middle Bronze, hitherto unrecognized, in Ammon and Moab. The line of Chedorlaomer's march was, therefore, exceedingly important during the Patriarchal Age.

P. 159 f. In connection with the question of the desert background of the Ark and the Tabernacle cf. the discussions of Arabic parallels, both pre-Islamic and modern, by R. Hartmann, ZAW 37, 219 ff., Lammens, *Le culte des bétyles (Bull. de l'Inst. d'Arch. Orient. du Caire,* Vol. 17), Morgenstern, *Heb. Union Col. Ann.,* Vol. 5, p. 81 ff.

P. 174. The writer now has additional material of importance for the study of the seals of the Temple Treasury, and expects to discuss the matter elsewhere soon.

P. 185, n. 69. See now Badè, *Some Tombs of Tell en-Nasbeh*, Berkeley, 1931.

P. 189, n. 102. See also *Bull. of the Am. School of Preh. Research*, April, 1931, p. 5 ff.

P. 189, n. 103. For Neuville's work in Wâdî Khreiṭûn see his paper *l'Acheuléen supérieur de la Grotte d'Oumm Qatafa (Palestine)* in *l'Anthropologie*, Vol. 41 (1931), pp. 13 ff., 249 ff.

P. 190, n. 5. See now the writer's paper, " The Third Campaign at Tell Beit Mirsim," JPOS, 1931, 105–129.

P. 197, n. 81. The view that the principal phase of the Conquest fell about 1400 B. C. is now elaborately defended by Garstang in his *Foundations of Bible History*, 1931, and will be maintained by Olmstead in his forthcoming *History of Palestine and Syria*.

P. 210, n. 30. It is true that the name is spelled in the vocabularies *Tirqan HURSAG* instead of *Tirqan KUR*, but the adjacent reference to " Southern Tirqan " makes it clear that the original was *Tirqan shadî*, " eastern Tirqan," which could be written in either way by a scribe who was careless of the meaning.

P. 211, n. 36. See against this position Dhorme, RB 1931, 506 ff. Dhorme upholds the antiquated combination of Amraphel with Hammurabi and of Arioch with Rim-Sin, by assuming that the source of Genesis XIV was in cuneiform, and supposing that some scribe wrote *Ammurabi* (with two orthographic peculiarities never found in early texts), which was then misread as *Ammurapil*, and that the name *Rim-Sin* was erroneously pronounced *Rim-Aku, Riwaku, Eriwaku*. Quite aside from the exceedingly improbable supposition that any source of this chapter was written in cuneiform, we find our imagination taxed to the limit to admit such extraordinary scribal errors. Moreover, Dhorme does not render his opponents the courtesy of describing their views correctly. His treatment of the historical topography of Palestine does not refer to anything done in this field outside of the École Biblique, despite the great importance of some of it. On the other hand, his earlier articles in the series *Abraham dans le cadre de l'histoire* (RB 1928, 367 ff., 481 ff., 1931, 364 ff.), which do not deal with specifically Palestinian matters at all, are accurate accounts of the cuneiform material bearing on Ur, Harran, the Aramæans, etc., in all periods, but avoid the treatment of basic problems.

P. 215, n. 71. Add the extremely suggestive book of Jirku's pupil, Schmökel, *Das angewandte Recht im Alten Testament*, Leipzig, 1930.

P. 215, n. 75. Iron was also found in Gilead, but the mines there never possessed any special importance.

P. 218, n. 97. Torrey continues to carry out his whole-sale reconstruction of exilic and post-exilic history in his *Pseudo-Ezekiel*, New Haven, 1930. In our opinion this brilliant study, which carries his theory to a new logical conclusion, is entirely erroneous. Cf. Budde, JBL 1931, 20 ff.

P. 222, n. 113. For the results of the first campaign at Beth-zur, under the auspices of the American School of Oriental Research in Jerusalem and the Presbyterian Theological Seminary of Chicago, and directed by O. R. Sellers, with the writer's assistance, see *Bulletin*, No. 43, October, 1931. The evidence for a break at the time of the Exile was quite clear so far as it went, but owing to the scarcity of clear stratification at this site was not extensive enough for definitive proof.

INDEX

(The references are selected, and material from the notes is only included when it cannot be found by reference to the corresponding page in the body of the book.)